**By The Editors of Consumer Guide**®

# 1957 CARS

CASTLE BOOKS

# CONTENTS

---

Copyright © 1980 by Publications International, Ltd.
All rights reserved
This book may not be reproduced or quoted in whole
or in part by mimeograph or any other printed means
or for presentation on radio or television without
written permission from:
Louis Weber, President
Publications International, Ltd.
3841 West Oakton Street
Skokie, Illinois 60076
Permission is never granted for commercial purposes.

Manufactured in the United States of America
1 2 3 4 5 6 7 8 9 10

Library of Congress Catalog Card Number: 80-81968
ISBN: 0-89009-375-4

This edition published by:
Castle Books
A Division of Book Sales, Inc.
110 Enterprise Avenue
Secaucus, N.J. 07094

Chief Contributing Author: Richard M. Langworth
Contributing Authors: Jeffrey I. Godshall, Walter E.
Gosden, Gwilym G. Griffiths, Roy A. Schneider

Cover Design: Frank E. Peiler

Photo Credits: American Motors Corp.; Chrysler
Historical Collection, Chrysler Corp.; Ford Photomedia
Service, Ford Motor Co.; Clark Gantree, DeSoto Club;
General Motors Corp.: Buick Division, Cadillac
Division, Chevrolet Division, Oldsmobile Division;
Pontiac Division; Jeffrey I. Godshall; Richard M.
Langworth; Richard Quinn, Studebaker; NASCAR;
National Automotive Historical Collection of the
Detroit Public Library.

Editorial Consultants: Jeffrey I. Godshall (Chrysler
Corporation section); Richard M. Langworth (American
Motors Corporation section and Studebaker-Packard
section); Hal Watts (Ford Motor Company section).

# INTRODUCTION

AMERICANS WHO were teen-agers in 1957 may not understand why many Americans really do not remember this vintage year at all. It was exactly that: a fine twelve months for the USA.

In those days, drivers went their way blissfully unaware of future gasoline shortages, Arab oil embargoes, automotive emissions, passive restraint systems and even safety belts (although belts were gradually winning acceptance and safety was on the mind of more than one manufacturer). While not an all-time record year, '57 was a period of success for most car producers, and a time of turnaround in the fortunes of hitherto unprofitable American Motors.

This was the year that Detroit took stock of the vast changes it had wrought in 1955, swept away most of its facelifted 1956 models, and brought out numerous dramatic-looking cars with a host of "new" engineering and performance innovations from pushbutton automatic transmission to air suspension. Styling saw hood and fenderlines merge into one plane, beltlines drop, glass areas increase, fins sprout or grow taller. The products of no two companies looked very much alike, although '57 was perhaps the last year when this was considered desirable. Today, you cannot tell a Plymouth from a Chevy without reading the labels or the plastic medallions. In 1957, you had only to glance at the cars from a distance.

In this present age of look-alike cars, it is pleasant to remember the variety—not only in styling but in make, size, price, trim, utility and performance—that was offered in 1957. Buyers still had the products of four great names among independents to choose from: Packard, Hudson, Nash and Studebaker. There was a compact contender, the Rambler, now offered with a 250 cubic-inch V8 as well as a penny-pinching Six. There were impressive luxury cars such as Cadillac Eldorados, Continental Mark IIs, Chrysler Imperials and Imperial Limousines by Ghia; personal luxury cars such as the two-seat Thunderbird and Studebaker Hawks; and an all-American sports car in the Chevrolet Corvette. Traditional top-sellers, Chevrolet, Ford and Plymouth, produced some of their best designed, hottest performing models in history in 1957: the beautiful and fleet Plymouth Fury, the Chevy Nomad wagon and the Ford Skyliner retractable hardtop. Virgil Exner introduced the all-new cars of the Forward Look at Chrysler; GM redesigned its Cadillacs, Buicks and Oldsmobiles; Ford fully revised its Lincoln, Mercury and Ford lines; Studebaker-Packard eliminated the Packards of old but produced the interesting Packard Clipper and the supercharged Golden Hawk. From Detroit to South Bend, Dearborn to Kenosha, it was a very good year for people who liked cars.

Although 1957 brought in many so-called "new features," history tells us that most had been around a long time. Fuel injection, which was offered by GM, had been in use by Mercedes-Benz and Indy racing cars since World War II. Pushbutton transmission, a Chrysler highlight, could be traced as far back as the 1918 Premiere. Gas turbines—Chrysler prototypes using production car bodies and the GM XP-500—only demonstrated a principle that had been in use on steamers since the turn of the century. The 12-volt electrical system, standard on most 1957 automobiles, had been commonplace on European cars since 1910. Power brakes were big on 1957, but LaSalle had offered them 20 years earlier; torsion bars were hailed as a revolution in suspension, yet the Leyland Eight had used them in 1921; the four-door hardtop was in its third year as a Detroit production body style, but a four-door hardtop without centerposts had been created by the Rohr Company in 1934.

Historical antecedents aside, 1957 was a significant year for the American automobile and, in retrospect, for the car collector of today. Chrysler hit an all-time styling peak—the last time Chrysler styling led instead of copied. Ford's retractable was the ultimate gadget car, its Mark II Continental the ultimate in luxury. Studebaker built what many feel was the best Hawk ever in 1957; the Clipper was the most luxurious Studebaker ever. GM's Eldorado Brougham was the Mark II's challenger; its fuel injection 'Vettes, Chevys and Bonnevilles were wonderful new performance ideas.

The Rambler Rebel with its big V8 was a performance surprise; and the 1957 Nash, if not the Hudson, was an attractive road car. There were "limited production" supercars from almost everybody, with custom trim and extra high-performance as standard. They included: Dodge's D-500, Cadillac's Eldorado, Mercury's Turnpike Cruiser, DeSoto's Adventurer, Buick's Roadmaster 75, Pontiac's Bonneville and Chrysler's 300-C.

This book examines in detail the offerings of Detroit 20 years ago, with a view not only of their history but also with a look at their attributes for the collector and enthusiast. In truth, many '57s already are "collector's items."

So if, after a look through these pages, you go out and find a nice '57 to add sparkle to your garage, we won't blame you.

Six million people did the same thing 20 years ago.

# AMERICAN MOTORS CORPORATION

AMERICAN MOTORS reported a loss for the fourth consecutive year in 1957, having made no money at all since George Mason of Nash-Kelvinator and A. Edward Barit of Hudson merged their companies in April, 1954. This time the loss was only $12 million—it had been a lot higher—on sales of $362 million. Nevertheless, many executives predicted that the crunch was over and that by 1958, AMC would record a dramatic turnaround.

"Big George" Mason first approached Barit about a merger in 1948. Barit was making money selling everything he could build then, and he demurred. Mason, one of the few independent company executives to see the future with blinders off, realized that in the long run the postwar independents could not stand against the might of GM, Ford and Chrysler. Unfortunately—for Packard, Studebaker, Nash and Hudson would have been a formidable combination right after the war—Mason had few disciples at the time. Most of his colleagues preferred to continue building their unique cars and trust that the future would provide for itself.

By 1953, though, it was a different story. Hudson sales had been declining rapidly for three years, the seller's market had turned to a buyer's, and Barit was looking at the future more realistically. In June, he and Mason had a series of meetings with their senior advisors. Big George said afterward, "He is tougher than hell. I have traded with (Charles W.) Nash for a good many years. I thought he was tough. But this guy Barit, he has a heart of stone! (Nevertheless) it has been a very pleasant negotiation. I think it is quite remarkable that we should arrive at a basis of exchange which would be acceptable to both shareholders." For Hudson shareholders, that last statement was charity. Merge was the only thing they could do.

## Mason's Dream

MASON HAD hoped for more than Hudson. His postwar dream, realized so early and before its time, saw all four major independents combine to cover all portions of the market, going toe to toe with the Big Three on an even basis. The name of Mason's dream company, even in the early days, was to have been American Motors. That much, at least, came true.

Mason's game plan was first stalled by his inability to convince Studebaker's Paul G. Hoffman and Harold Vance that anything profitable could come of combining rivals like Nash (builder of the economy Rambler) with Studebaker (builder of the economy Champion). According to Packard's James J. Nance, Mason tried to get around this problem by asking Nance to take on Packard, merge it with Studebaker, then fold in with Mason-merged Nash-Hudson. Nance did absorb Studebaker, but the whole idea came crashing down after Mason's death in October 1954.

George Romney was Mason's hand-picked successor, and Romney would not play. For whatever reasons (he has never granted an interview about his AMC days), Romney disdained Studebaker-Packard. There are several possible reasons why. He was not known for getting along famously with Nance, and the question of who would head the combined four companies could have been thorny. Also, Studebaker was in far worse financial condition by 1954 than even Nance realized; perhaps Romney had some information that Packard's president did not. The biggest reason surely was Romney's decision to concentrate on the Rambler—a policy of foresight. The Rambler had begun to move by 1954 or 1955, and its potential was great. It was the only small car to have achieved

*Only 1500 high-performance Rambler Rebels, such as the four-door, were made in 1957.*

success: the Henry J. Aero-Willys and Hudson Jet had all failed miserably. Rambler was, therefore, the only car left in a market sector completely missed by the Big Three. On October 12, 1954, Romney proclaimed "no merger discussions" with S-P, without mentioning whether there had ever been any talks with Studebaker or Packard separately."We are highly diversified," he said. "We know we have a bright and prosperous future as American Motors. It is not based on merger with any other company." In short order Romney scrapped the interchange program of Packard engines for minor AMC components that had begun under the Mason regime, and Studebaker-Packard had to go its own way.

Under Romney, AMC went to work to eliminate duplication of product or facilities. Dealers were gradually integrated, and all were given Ramblers to sell. The last "Step-down" Hudsons were completed in late 1954 and the Hudson plant on Jefferson Avenue in Detroit was sold. Hudson manufacture moved to Nash country—Kenosha, Wisconsin—and the 1955 Hudson used a Nash unit body/chassis. In due course even this duplication was eliminated by dropping the big Hudsons and Nashes entirely.

**Rambler All Alone**

INSTEAD OF AMC's strongest seller, Rambler became its only seller. For 1955 the corporation built

194,000 cars, of which about 84,000 were Ramblers. By 1957, Rambler production had risen to 114,000 out of 119,000 for a 96 percent share. Except for the tiny Metropolitan that was imported from England, Rambler was the only make in the 1958 AMC line. By 1957 the company was into its third million unit-body cars, and the Kenosha production line was rapidly expanding.

George Romney put a personal stamp on the Rambler sales drive with one of the most aggressive campaigns ever seen in Detroit. Publicly accusing his rivals of building "gas hogs" and "trundling tanks," Romney took to the air waves, print media, dealer conferences and trade journals to promote the sense and value of his short-wheelbase small car. With single-minded intensity he dropped the sporting Nash-Healey and forgot the potential new generation Hudson offered by the 1954-55 Italia and X-161. (Mason had already talked Barit out of continuing the dowdy Hudson Jet.) He kept the Metropolitan going because it fitted the economy image. American Motors managed to survive a difficult 1956 without dipping below 100,000 cars or losing more than $20 million.

In 1957 Romney back-pedaled a bit by offering a V8 Rambler, but it was not really a change in policy. The car's engine was only 250 cubic inches, probably the stingiest fuel sipper ever produced among V8s. It broadened AMC's market territory with a performance option—public admission that compact size might be a desirable characteristic all by itself. In a way, Romney was breaking early ground for the "personal" small cars that appeared in the early Sixties.

### Romney's "X-Ray"

ONE OF ROMNEY'S more controversial ideas was *X-Ray,* a little booklet purporting to present facts about the Rambler and its competition. It was a typically biased sales pitch, but one of the most successful. Rambler sales responded 114,000 in 1957 and 217,000 in 1958, which was a recession year for the rest of the industry. In 1959 Romney built over 400,000 cars—more than any year of Nash and Hudson combined—and by 1960 Rambler was the third-place car in production, displacing Plymouth with close to half a million vehicles.

Unfortunately, AMC failed to retain its position in the late Sixties and Seventies. When Romney left to pursue politics, his successors drifted back to the "full line" approach in another vain attempt to meet the Big Three in all market sectors. The economy car boom turned into a sporty car boom, and Rambler's market was diluted after the arrival of Big Three compacts in late 1959. Despite cars like the 1957 Rebel, AMC never seemed able to shake its Nash Rambler image.

In 1957, however, AMC was on the threshold of its greatest years. It offered a line of competitively priced, nicely finished Ramblers with a useful choice of powerplants, along with the unique Metropolitan and a waning line of large Hudsons and Nashes. Ironically, the latter are the main interest of collectors today; in 1957 they were very much second fiddle to the Rambler.

AMC's success through its one-model policy for 1957 is in some contrast to Studebaker-Packard, which in the same year offered a broad line of cars and took a predictable beating. The survival of AMC, and the demise of S-P ten years hence, can be laid partly to this difference of approach during 1957.

# HUDSON

FOR THE HUDSON automobile, 1957 was the final curtain. After nearly half a century, the car named for a Detroit department store magnate who put up most of the money (but provided little expertise) for the company's founding in 1908 was dropped from the market by American Motors. The cars were facelifted 1956 models, which themselves were facelifted 1955s, on a body that had originated in 1952.

The 1955-57 period marks the era of what some Hudson partisans call the "Hash"—Nash-based cars with special Hudson trim, identification and, sometimes, engines. The first Hash, in 1955, was a thoroughly well-styled car, imaginative and different from its Nash counterpart. In 1956, however, AMC stylist Edmund E. Anderson brought in what was called "V-line Styling," an attempt to bring back Hudson's old triangular emblem motif. He may have brought it back, but the overall effect was so gaudy that even 1956 buyers found Hudsons a bit pretentious. Anderson's styling extended into 1957 because AMC could not afford to change it. If a 1958 Hudson had been built, it would have been constructed on the new 117-inch wheelbase Rambler Ambassador chassis. For a time there was some thought of applying the Nash and Hudson names to the Ambassador line.

Hudson cars had been undergoing shakeups ever since the Nash merger, as AMC tried to resolve its financial and model-lineup dilemmas. In 1954 the last of the old Step-down Hudsons and compact Jets (a notoriously unsuccessful although well-engineered compact) had departed. In 1955 the Nash-based Hudsons debuted along with Hudson-labeled Ramblers and Metropolitans. Over

## 1957 Hudson Specifications

| Make and Model | Dimensions | | | | Engines | |
| | Wheelbase ins. | Overall Length ins. | Overall Width ins. | Overall Height ins. | 327 cu. in. V8 255 Bhp. | Weight lbs. |
| --- | --- | --- | --- | --- | --- | --- |
| Hornet | 121.3 | 209.3 | 78 | 60.4 | S | 3539 |

**Key:** S: *Standard Engine*

*The exterior styling of the Hudson Hornet Hollywood was merely a revamping of a previous facelift. Hudsons were the only '57 cars with fins on the front as well as rear fenders.*

25,000 Hudson Ramblers and Mets were sold, but the Ramblers had such a good year overall that AMC elected to build them as a separate marque for 1957. Both Hudson and Nash dealers continued to sell them, but the individual Hudson and Nash badges were dropped. This was a sensible alteration, because even the factory did not distinguish between the two and often changed the make by switching badges depending on the order backlog.

**Line Shrinks**

BY THE TIME 1956 rolled around, Hudson was down to eight Wasp and Hornet models with three different engines. In 1957, with Rambler sales even stronger, the Hudson line was down to four Hornets: the Super and Custom, in four-door sedan and Hollywood hardtop guise. The engine in all cases was the new 327 cubic-inch AMC V8, producing 255 horsepower and 345 pounds-feet of torque. It featured standard four-barrel carburetion, dual exhausts and aluminum alloy slipper-type pistons.

Other mechanical selling points of the '57 Hudsons included 12-volt electrics, Torque Tube drive, duo servo brakes, Weather-Eye heating and ventilation, 14-inch wheels and a suspension change: Hudson switched from kingpin-type front suspension to a steering knuckle assembly which pivoted on antifriction bearings to make steering easier and smoother.

Styling changes for 1957 amounted to half-hearted attempts to keep up with the times. Three-tone paint jobs were offered on the Customs: a common combination was metallic avocado lower and black upper body, with light cream top. Hudson had grafted fins onto its rear fenders in 1956, which were modified slightly in 1957; it also tried to one-up everybody else in '57 by putting them on the front fenders as well. The result was a pair of twin-bladed fins that looked as out of place as they really were.

To emphasize the V8 engine there was a new "V" medallion in the center of the grille. Side trim included an anodized aluminum or painted accent panel on the front fenders and doors. Hudson emphasized "personalized" cars by offering a total of 32 color combinations and luxurious interiors: three-toned in metallic weave nylon, vinyl or leather. On Supers, two-tone or solid paint were available, but three-tones were not. Typical of the period, the lower-priced Super was a cleaner-looking car than the Custom; also typical was that more Customs were sold than Supers.

Sales features which had always recommended Nash cars were still in evidence on the 1957 Hudson. Single-unit construction, with body and frame members welded together to form one integral unit, provided safety and quiet operation. Nash's patented reclining seats were a Hudson option, while its 16-inch-wide rear center armrest, pullout drawer-type glovebox, ashtrays and radio speakers at each side of the dash, padded sun visors and

The 1957 Hudson Hornet V8, including the four-door sedan, was covered with V-shaped trim.

color-keyed interiors were all standard. Power brakes were standard on the Hornet Custom and optional on the Super. Air conditioning was available for the first time, this being one of the things the old independent Hudson company never got around to.

## Obvious Trend

WITH AMC producing 96 Ramblers to every four Hudsons and Nashes, the trend of the future was obvious. However, the automotive industry was expecting a 1958 Hudson as late as September 1957, allegedly with over 300 hp extracted from the 327 V8 and air suspension optional. Rumor promised better utilization of interior space and dual headlights (only Nash offered them in 1957), as well as a Hudson station wagon (which would have been the first since before World War II), as well as a two-door sedan. The sketches purporting to predict the 1957 Hudson turned out to be the 1958 Rambler Ambassador.

According to several sources at American Motors, there was a lot of soul-searching about the decision to drop the Hudson name. According to contemporary newspaper reports, at least one executive was unhappy about it. A. E. Barit, his son says, was "terribly disappointed in the merge, but he felt it was necessary to the survival of Hudson." Barit departed the board at around this time, and some say he did so because of the decision to drop the Hudson marque. Roy Chapin, present AMC

board chairman and a director at the time, disputes this. Barit, Chapin says, was "always a realist." One newspaper reported that the last car Barit owned was a Hudson built by American Motors. When that car went out of service, Barit never bought another.

Roy Chapin summarized the decision that eliminated both the Hudson/Nash Ramblers in 1956 and Hudson and Nash themselves in 1957: "We had run Hudson and Nash Metropolitans and Ramblers for a year—it was a charade. They were basically the exact same automobiles, and the decision really was one that said we have got to spend our money and our effort and our concentration on the Rambler because we have not got enough dough to update the big Nashes and the big Hudsons. So the final decision was to get it all behind one name and not try to advertise two different automobiles when they really are one. That is a simple explanation for a basic corporate decision that said we have got to put this whole thing together into one package."

The 1955-57 Hudsons have a lot to recommend them in the way of engineering, and the 1955 Hudson was well styled. The same cannot be said about the 1957 Hudson. It was ugly, dated and garish. On the other hand, it was a big, comfortable car, a fine highway automobile and the last of a great line. This is what qualifies it as a collector's item. Other companies built even uglier cars in 1957; they are not collected widely today. The "Hash" is collected because it was the very last Hudson. Although AMC revived the name Hornet in 1970, Hudson, after this one, was gone for good.

# NASH

WHATEVER Edmund Anderson felt about Hudson did not apply to brother Nash. Compared to the '57 Hudson, the Nash, using the exact same body, was outstanding. It was a beautiful facelift of a six-year-old body that kept this big AMC car up-to-date for one more year. It turned out to be its last year.

"The World's Newest, Finest Travel Car!" was the way Nash billed the 1957 Ambassador. Like Hudson's Wasp, the junior Statesman had been dropped, so the aura of the top-line model could apply throughout the range. There was a lot new about the Ambassador, especially the extensive restyling.

Nash had been hobbling along with inboard-mounted headlights in 1955 and 1956, apparently more as a styling trick than to serve any function. In 1957 Nash got them out on the fenders again, and simultaneously introduced the first four-headlamp system on a volume automobile. This was a dead heat with the Eldorado Brougham. Both Nash and Brougham appeared late and were able to take advantage of changed headlamp standards in the various states. Cadillac built only 400 Broughams in '57. AMC built 10,330 Nashes. It is strange that this Nash is not more widely collected and displayed by today's enthusiasts. If a grand old marque had to go, this was not a bad way for it to end.

The "four eyes" were what made Nash styling so up-to-date, abetted by very careful facelifting. Full wheel cutouts finally succeeded the peculiar half-hidden wheelhousings of 1952-56. The grille was a latticework oval, understated and indented. It bore a "V" medallion to remind people of the AMC V8 engine, and a Nash medallion for the last time on a passenger car. A trace of tinsel was apparent in the old-fashioned fender-top parking lights. Nash went Buick one better in '57 by placing not one but two chrome bullets inside a ring to form the hood ornament.

## Typical of Era

THE 1957 NASH is a good example of that peculiar facet of Eisenhower Age styling: the cheaper models look better today than the top-line ones do. The latter were often over-decorated and therefore did not wear as well visually. In Nash's case, the Ambassador Super (ex-Statesman) lacked the broad "lightning bolt" two-tone panel of the Ambassador Custom. As a result, it was remarkably chrome-free, with its two-toning restricted to the roof. Both models used a new and attractive taillight design: a large extended red oval at the top visible from all three sides, and a hefty back-up light lens running vertically underneath. Unlike Hudson, Nash avoided bolt-on weld-on fins in 1957, and looked far better as a result. The "Continental" exterior spare tire mount was a popular option and improved the looks of the cars by extending their length.

Together with its energetic facelift in '57, Nash ran off a giant's handful of new features which suggested that the car might still be around in '58. "If it is New, Nash Has It," wrote the admen. The four beam headlights, they said, provided 150 watts and more light at higher levels; the Lightning Streak, they said, exemplified "the swift sweep of racing line." There were luxurious new fabrics, vinyls and leathers, and the widest front seat ever built into a production automobile. Shoulder room and headroom were on the Cadillac scale. There were dual exhausts, a transistor-powered radio and center-mounted slide-out glovebox. There were all the traditional Nash features: safety padded instrument panel and sun visors; optional reclining seats; deep coil-spring suspension on all four wheels; and the world's best heating and ventilating system, Nash Weather-Eye, which even GM coveted. Seat belt publicity returned and belts could be installed by dealers.

The big push was Nash's patented single-unit

## 1957 Nash Specifications

| Make and Model | Dimensions | | | | Engines | |
| | Wheelbase ins. | Overall Length ins. | Overall Width ins. | Overall Height ins. | 327 cu. in. V8 255 Bhp. | Weight lbs. |
|---|---|---|---|---|---|---|
| Ambassador | 121.3 | 209.3 | 78 | 60.4 | S | 3597 |

**Key:** *S: Standard Engine*

*Of the two Nash lines offered in 1957, the Super was the plainest. It lacked the two-tone panel of the Custom and flaunted less chrome. The 1957 Nash Ambassador Super was available as a two-door hardtop (1) and as a four-door sedan (2). The Ambassador Custom models were offered in the same two- and four-door versions.*

construction, "the pattern of cars to come" according to brochures. "You owe your loved ones the protection of AMC Double Safe Single-Unit Construction," exhorted the ads. "This is the greatest safety feature ever built into an automobile." In ordinary cars, Nash said, the body was bolted to a separate chassis frame, mounting the passengers above its protection. The AMC body, on the other hand, featured "extended frame girders at the front, sides, top and rear, forming a steel box girder enclosure that gives true wraparound protection—twice as safe as other cars. Some day all cars will be built this better way." They are not, at least not all; but more are being built that way than ever before, so Nash was indeed pointing the way in '57.

## Ambassador Power

THE AMBASSADOR used the 327 V8 with four-barrel carburetor and dual exhausts as standard equipment. The 255 hp engine had been introduced late in 1956 with 240 horsepower. It was conventional, but soundly designed and efficient. Attached to the unit body on four mounts, the 327 used aluminum alloy, steel-insert three-ring pistons; five main-bearing crank; and cast-iron cylinder heads. It was designed by David Potter. A point of interest is that it might have first appeared in 1954, on a Kaiser Manhattan.

"Some of the design ideas of the proposed Kaiser 288 cubic-inch-displacement V8 did become

the industry design some years later," Potter said recently. "Whether this was carried by Kaiser engineers to other companies when Kaiser closed or was just the natural progress of the best way is hard to say. Some design ideas I used in the AMC V8 are found in all modern designs: green sand casting (instead of baked oil sand core) for the tappet chamber and front face to achieve greater dimensional accuracy as well as low foundry cost, for example."

This engine was a big improvement on the 250 cubic-inch unit introduced earlier, the V8 applied in 1957 to the Rambler. The latter had powered a Hudson to 60 from rest in only 14.5 seconds and scored 69.7 miles per hour in 19.7 seconds in the

quarter mile. The new V8 was greatly improved, with 0-60 times in the 12-second range and a quarter-mile ability on the order of 80 mph in 18 seconds.

**End of the Name**

MANY FELT the name of Nash should have been preserved on the larger Ramblers. Of the two firms, Nash was probably the more qualified to survive, because its resources at merger time were much larger than Hudson's. The change was felt necessary in order to allow sales to push Ramblers, which were almost certainly the only way to succeed in the passenger car field. Furthermore, market surveys showed that people liked and related to the Rambler name, which had been around longer than either Nash or Hudson.

Ambassador, of course, survived in 1958 and beyond: first as a Rambler model; later as an AMC make. The Statesman had disappeared with the Hudson Wasp in 1956. The Hornet name was dropped after 1957, to appear again on a new AMC compact in 1970.

Of all the Farina-styled Nashes from 1952 through 1957, the last were almost certainly the best. Coupled with Nash's famous long-haul com-forts including reclining seats and all-coil spring suspension, they offered the most powerful engine ever to power a Nash car. Yet the engines were reasonably sized and returned decent fuel econo-my, especially with three-speed manual shift or overdrive. The proclivity of the unit body to rust, as well as the small number of Nashes produced, make the '57 one of the rarer models. Especially rare is the Super with its quiet styling. Over the road they were some of the most supremely comfortable cars of their day. Despite their rarity, they do not cost much in the collector market now.

# RAMBLER/METROPOLITAN

THE 1957 RAMBLER line was one of the more interesting, thanks to the Rebel. The limited-production four-door hardtop was painted silver, with gold-anodized side trim and special iden-tification. This flashy decoration served to an-nounce AMC's 327 cubic-inch V8 which was in-stalled for the first time in a Rambler. Other models offered a 250 cubic-inch V8. The results of the 327 were as outstanding as they were unexpected. The Rebel proved that AMC cars could go, as well as save.

Rebels were fitted with adjustable Gabriel shocks on all four corners, a track rod to minimize roll, heavy-duty springs, power steering and brakes, padded sun visors and dash, and most minor ac-cessories. Bendix fuel injection was planned, but did not materialize. The Rebel engine remained the same as was used in the big Nashes and Hudsons at 255 horsepower, although compression was raised to 9.5:1. The difference, of course, was in weight: while the big cars' pounds/hp ratio was on the order of 14.5:1, the Rebel's was only 13:1. The difference made for great performance.

AMC brought a Rebel to Daytona Beach, Florida, in early 1957. Joe H. Wherry, an automotive writer who drove it, had these comments: "From scratch, the Rebel made 60 miles per hour (true) in an average of 7.5 seconds with the writer only aboard (with three aboard, best time was 7.8). From a steady 50 mph in overdrive, the needle hits a cor-rected 80, with sudden kickdown slapping the box back into third in just 7.2 seconds. That is high performance, believe me, when family cars are un-der discussion."

Wherry continued "Handling is fine—not superb, but improved over the regular Rambler line . . . [the suspension components] minimize roll, make nose-diving on fast stops very slight indeed, and prevent bottoming except in cases where speed is extreme. The torque tube drive line prevents rear axle wind-up on fast takeoffs. Feel of the road is good, even with power steering (Gemmer), al-though the lock is too great (nearly four turns)."

Wherry noted some brake fade on repeated ap-plications from high speeds. "But, the Rebel sho-'nuff ain't the only power packed critter with brakes that need beefing up, by any means."

### Facelift for '57

THE RAMBLER had been completely revamped by AMC styling for 1956. Its former Nash-like lines had been replaced by a squarer, more chiseled body

## 1957 Rambler Specifications

| Make and Model | Dimensions | | | | Engines | | |
|---|---|---|---|---|---|---|---|
| | Wheelbase ins. | Overall Length ins. | Overall Width ins. | Overall Height ins. | 250 cu. in. V8 192 Bhp | 196 cu. in. Six 125 Bhp | Weight lbs. |
| Rambler V8 | 108 | 191.2 | 71.3 | 58 | S | — | 3179 |
| Rambler Six | 108 | 191.2 | 71.3 | 58 | — | S | 2891 |

**Key:** *S: Standard Engine*

with fashionably wrapped windshield and inboard-mounted headlights with fender-mounted running lamps. A new four-door hardtop body style was available both as a sedan and Cross Country wagon. It was not a particularly memorable design, but one typical of the era. The 1956 models had been three-toned, but in 1957 the color spectrum was limited to two different tones maximum, and they were more modest in configuration: the second color was applied to a band along the sides of the car.

Aside from the Rebel's 327 V8, Ramblers of the regular series were available with AMC's smaller 250 cubic-inch unit, producing 190 brake horsepower at 4900 rpm. The 250 used a fully counterbalanced crankshaft and two-barrel carburetor. Its arrival signified that AMC was concentrating on the Rambler line more than ever before, and that in contrast with the past, it would broaden Rambler's appeal from strictly economy to economy-plus-performance. The 250 was small, efficient and able to record 20-plus miles per gallon economy while greatly adding to Rambler performance.

Minor engineering news was the use of variable-wedge combustion chambers in the Rambler Six. Through compression and carburetion changes, the Six was up to 125 to 135 horsepower. Ramblers used 12-volt electrics, as did their larger AMC cousins, and offered optional Airliner reclining seats. Like Nash, Rambler used all-coil spring suspension. Its 20-gallon fuel tank provided a long cruising range. Torque tube drive and nine-inch diameter brakes also were borrowed from Nash, as were the transmission options of manual, overdrive and Hydra-matic. The option list included power

## 1957 Metropolitan Specifications

| Make and Model | Dimensions | | | | Engines | |
| --- | --- | --- | --- | --- | --- | --- |
| | Wheelbase ins. | Overall Length ins. | Overall Width ins. | Overall Height ins. | 91 cu. in. OH4 52 Bhp | Weight lbs. |
| Metropolitan | 85 | 149.5 | 61.5 | 54.5 | S | 1875 |

**Key:** *S: Standard Engine*

steering at $59; and air conditioning at only $345, which was a fairly low price 20 years ago for what was then a rather new auto accessory.

### Longer Wheelbase

LIKE THE 1956s, the 1957 Ramblers used a 108-inch wheelbase instead of the 100-inch that had been the norm since introduction in 1950. The 100-inch wheelbase cars were dropped only for 1957, however; in 1958, they returned as the Rambler American, expanding the line downward into even more compact territory. The American, still in its original Farina-Nash body style, lasted until 1961, when it was completely revised. The 100-inch wheelbase survived through 1963. It ran up a 14-year career that saw it break new ground as the

*A larger, 1500cc engine boosted the Metropolitan's horsepower to 52 in 1957. This was an increase of 24 percent over previous models. Fuel economy ranged up to 40 mpg.*

pioneer compact, help establish Rambler's reputation for economy, and endear the little beast to the American public in hitherto unprecedented numbers.

The Rambler line of Sixes and V8s was priced cleverly, just a few dollars above the cheapest Fords and Chevrolets from $1961 (Deluxe Six) to over $2700 (Rebel or hardtop Cross Country). At these prices, AMC was able to offer a slightly more luxurious car than Big Three rivals and cover its higher per-unit overhead at Kenosha. The fact that AMC lost money in 1957 was not the fault of the Rambler, which was going from strength to strength. There were other, lingering problems: expenses from the merger, the nonprofitability of the big cars, the costs of abandoning Hudson's

Detroit plant, and similar factors still to be dealt with. Thanks to Rambler, however, AMC sales were up 10,000 units at the end of the year, and from that point, the firm proceeded to record one production record after another.

Only about 1500 Rebels were produced, so these models did not significantly contribute to output. The regular V8 and Six were each assigned to six individual models, but the V8 Ramblers were built as Supers and Customs only and not available in bottom-line Deluxe guise. A sole price leader comprised that series, a six cylinder four-door coming in at just under $2000. In the V8 area, the Custom was the most popular model, offered with both pillar and pillarless versions of the four-door sedan and wagon models.

▲ *The flat rear section of the Rambler Custom Cross Country's roof was ideal for mounting an accessory roof rack.*

*Only four-door Rambler Custom models were offered in 1957. The line included a hardtop (below), sedan*
▼ *and two wagons.*

## Popular Model

THE CROSS COUNTRY was Rambler's most popular 1956-57 innovation. It deserved its acclaim. Compared to wagons Rambler had offered through 1955, the CC boasted one-third more cargo capacity and increased seating room. It also introduced a feature that was to become widespread—a roll-down rear window that disappeared into the tailgate, eliminating the clumsy, dangerous upper tailgate which had plagued all steel wagons since the 1949 Plymouth. Cross Country styling was an attractive combination of sedan and wagon roofs: sedanlike to the rear door, where it broke contour and ran straight back, providing a platform for a chrome luggage rack. Cross Country Custom two-toning was in woodgrain rather than a contrasting color.

Correctly a make in its own right, but usually associated with Rambler, was the Metropolitan. It was offered with a larger 1500 cubic-centimeter engine of 52 horsepower in 1957. The Met 1500 was 24 percent more powerful than previous models and could be distinguished by its mesh-type grille and two-tone paint line in the form of an elongated "S" on body sides. Mets were available with soft top or hardtop: both models seated two people and were known for 40-mpg economy (as well as a tendency to rust). When production finally ended in 1962, AMC had built 94,986 of them. Of all small AMC products in 1957, they are the hottest among today's collectors.

*The most popular body style was the Cross Country wagon, shown here in 'Super form (1). It introduced a roll-down rear window that disappeared into the tailgate. It also featured sedan-like styling and two-tone exterior trim. The Rambler Deluxe Six (2) was priced just slightly above the lowest-cost Chevys and Fords.*

*This Chrysler Dart Experimental Car was built by Carrozzeria-Ghia of Torino, Italy, and was shown to the American public during 1957.*

**F**OR CHRYSLER Corporation, 1957 marked the end of an ambitious three-year struggle by its managers to win back the company's traditional 20 percent-plus share of the American car market. They almost made it.

Chrysler's 1957 cars were the result of a crisis three years earlier. The corporation from 1936 to 1950 had been the No. 2 producer of passenger cars in the United States, ahead of Ford Motor Company, with an average 23.7 percent of industry sales. But from 1950 through 1953 Chrysler watched itself slip to third place, behind a fast-rising Ford. Then in 1954, Chrysler experienced the

most disastrous year in its history. Its market share plunged to a paltry 13.2 percent, the lowest since 1931, while Ford's rose to 30.62 percent. Plymouth, long accustomed to having permanent possession of third place behind Chevy and Ford, fell to fifth; Dodge, DeSoto, and Chrysler all fell drastically. Suddenly, the industry giant saw itself not only losing its "rightful" share of the market but in real danger of becoming the junior partner in a "Big Two-and-a-Half."

The principal reason for the decline was the company's stodgy styling. Ever since the failure of the radical Airflow, Chrysler products had been

16

# CHRYSLER CORPORATION

conservatively styled; but because of their generally superior engineering and solid value, they had sold well despite the ho-hum styling. By 1954, however, the unglamorous, boxy, "bigger on the inside-smaller on the outside" cars and the lack of a fully automatic transmission on most of the company's lines put Chrysler in an extremely poor position against the hot V8 Fords and the completely redesigned Buick, Olds, and Cadillac from GM.

A horrified Chrysler management watched Buick capture third place while Buick and Olds together tore holes in Dodge and DeSoto sales. At the other end of the scale, the restyled Cadillac pushed ahead of Chrysler despite the Chrysler's position as the most powerful car in America. Stung by the company's rapid decline and a mounting dealer revolt, President L.L. "Tex" Colbert committed the company to a no-holds-barred three-year push to regain Chrysler's traditional slice of the market.

## Exner Styling

CHRYSLER HAD sensed that its styling was becoming old hat as early as 1949, when then-president K.T. Keller brought in Virgil Exner to head an advanced styling section. With a small select staff, Exner (formerly of GM and the Raymond Loewy/Studebaker staffs) turned out a spate of well-received show cars, yet he was not really allowed to influence the company's production cars until the 1955 models. When Chrysler's 1955 line—christened "The Forward Look"—debuted in November, 1954, all lines were bigger, longer, flashier, and dramatically two- and three-toned. Plymouth got a V8 and the now fully automatic Powerflite transmission was available across the board.

The Forward Look brought Chrysler a long way back toward recovery, but the success was not enough to regain third place for Plymouth or earn the corporation a 20 percent market share. However, the handsome profits and company-wide enthusiasm for styling and product innovation persuaded Chrysler that a radical product policy was its key to survival.

In 1956 Chrysler introduced "Flight Sweep" styling—fins—to the American public and the upswept tail became Chrysler's styling symbol. But '56 was a disappointing year for Chrysler, with production slipping again. Come 1957, there would be a different story.

On October 30, 1956, Chrysler unveiled the most dramatic cars in its 32-year history. All five lines were completely, totally new: Plymouth, Dodge, DeSoto, Chrysler, and Imperial were redesigned. It was the last year that Chrysler would redesign all of its cars at the same time. Their "New Shape of Motion" styling was nothing short of sensational. Hoods were smooth and flat and flush with the fenders; bodies were taut and eager; rears were unmistakable with proud and soaring fins. Light-looking roofs featured greatly increased glass area, and hardtops were inches lower. Beneath those flat hoods and flashy fins lay some of the industry's most powerful V8s and a new suspension system that set high standards for ride and handling.

## Three Major Goals

CHRYSLER OFFICIALS had three goals in 1957: to regain their company's 20 percent plus of the market, put Plymouth back in third place, and establish the Imperial as a separate car line. They almost brought it off.

Chrysler produced 1,296,063 cars in the 1957 model year as the company's share of the domestic market rose to 19.5 percent, most of which was taken from General Motors. GM now had an unenviable reputation for conservatively styled cars.

Although the corporation did not quite make the magic 20 percent mark, it did accomplish its two other objectives with a flourish. Plymouth produced 731,001 cars in 1957 compared with 615,532 in 1956 to move solidly ahead of Buick for third place. Chrysler was serious about Plymouth's position in the market. That was made clear in the summer of 1956 when 1300 field salesmen assembled in Detroit to preview the 1957 models. All top Chrysler officials from Tex Colbert on down wore big yellow lapel badges bearing the slogan "Plymouth is Our Number One Job."

One of Plymouth's marketing problems was its unique dealer setup. In 1930, Chrysler gave the Plymouth franchise to all its Dodge, DeSoto, and Chrysler dealers to help them ride out the depression. It worked, and overnight Plymouth had a huge selling body. But after World War II, the dualled dealers worked to Plymouth's disadvantage. When times were good, Dodge, DeSoto, and Chrysler dealers emphasized their higher-priced, higher-profit cars over the Plymouth. When times were bad, dealers found themselves selling Plymouths in direct competition with other Chrysler Corp. dealers across the street. Ford and Chevy did not have this problem. Their dealers were free to concentrate on selling one car line. Chrysler then began opening Plymouth-only dealerships in certain urban areas. There was tough talk from Chrysler brass that dealers had to sell Plymouth hard; if it sold, they said, the company's other car lines would take care of themselves. The campaign was successful: Plymouth regained and remained in third place until a wide-tracked, split-grilled Pontiac came along in the 1960s.

At the top of the market, Chrysler succeeded in establishing the Imperial as a serious competitor for Lincoln and Cadillac. In 1955, when the Imperial was split off from Chrysler and registered as a separate make, 11,432 were produced; 10,784 were produced in 1956. But in 1957, 37,557 cars were built. That was an all-time high for the marque and a record that still stood when the last Imperial came off the line in June, 1975. Imperial production reached 24.2 percent of Chrysler Division's total in 1957, compared with 11.3 percent in 1956. As a result of this spectacular performance, the Imperial was moved into its own plant in Dearborn in the summer of 1958.

### Revolutionary Look

THE LOOK of Chrysler's 1957 line was indeed revolutionary. One only had to park a 1957 Plymouth next to a 1954 model to see how far the corporation had come in a few short years. Thanks to Virgil Exner and his talented staff, Chrysler was now the undisputed styling leader of the industry. The cars were conceived to be three years ahead of the competition; that is, the kind of cars Chrysler would normally have been producing in 1960 had they not decided to advance their introduction to regain the company's lost ground. In fact, Plymouth used the advertising slogan "Suddenly it's 1960!" until public confusion about the car's actual model year resulted in the revamped phrase, "The 1957

Plymouth—Three Years Ahead!".

Key to the new styling was the dramatic, soaring tailfins. Today they may be considered decadent and ugly, but back then they had a great visual and emotional impact. Exner liked the high fins because the resulting dart-shaped silhouette made the hoods look low and gave the cars a look of forward motion. There was a lot of talk about their relationship to modern aircraft and racing boats, and wind tunnel tests showed that the high fins reduced steering effort up to 20 percent in strong crosswinds; but the real reason they were there was to distinguish Chrysler cars from the rest of the industry. They were daring and distinctive, and when often accompanied by dual fin-mounted aerials, they proclaimed in no uncertain way that these were the newest cars on the road.

Most people liked them. A magazine survey of Plymouth owners revealed that 64.2 percent liked the fins. The cars were low—startlingly so—with two-door hardtops more than five inches lower than their 1956 counterparts, and most Plymouth owners surveyed liked the extreme lowness as well.

The clean, wedge-shaped styling earned Chrysler the Gold Medal Award of the Industrial Design Institute; earned Exner a promotion to vice-president; and, more importantly, earned the dollars of the American car buyer.

Exner's fins really shook up the competition, especially GM. The story is told that soon after introduction, GM styling boss Harley Earl walked into the office of Chevrolet exterior head C.M. MacKichan, threw a '57 Plymouth catalog on his desk, and asked bitterly, "Why don't you quit?" Former GM designers remember all five Chrysler cars lined up in the GM styling showroom, engineers and stylists pouring over them. Earl was not about to be "out-finned" by Chrysler; GM's 1959 bat-wing Chevys, wedge-wing Buicks, and shark-fin Caddys were the result. Nothing Chrysler has done since has influenced mighty GM as much as those tail fins did.

### Engineering Developments

CHRYSLER PULLED some smart body tricks in '57. There was one set of bodies for Plymouth and Dodge, another for Chrysler and DeSoto, and a different one for the Imperial. All of the station wagons shared a single body design. There were many common parts.

Biggest news in the engineering department, however, was "Torsion-Aire" suspension. The system used torsion bars in front and a modified conventional system in the rear. Automotive writers for several of the leading magazines at the time gave the suspension rave reviews. The Plymouth was called "the most roadable car ever built in this country," the Imperial was touted as "the easiest handling car weighing over 2500 pounds," and *Motor Trend* awarded Chrysler for "superior handling and roadability in all its cars." The system was so successful that it is still used today in all of Chrysler's domestic cars.

Other improvements included smaller 14-inch wheels, bigger brakes and a greatly improved transmission. Heating and air conditioning systems were fully contained under the hood, eliminating outside air scoops and trunk-mounted components.

As for gasoline economy, Chrysler-built cars swept every class in the 1957 Mobilgas Economy Run, with each car averaging over 20 miles per gallon, and the Imperial emerged as the Sweepstakes Winner. It was a victory without precedent.

Designing, engineering and building the radical '57s strained the talents of the corporate staffs to their fullest. In fact, the new bodies caused too many problems and the quality of the '57s often was not good. Even so, 1957 was a very successful year for Chrysler. The cars sold well, won acclaim from the press and established the company as the industry leader in innovation.

# CHRYSLER/IMPERIAL

THE CHRYSLER for 1957 was perhaps the smoothest of the corporation's lineup. The car shared bodies with the senior DeSotos but featured a very graceful winged bumper and grille assembly. Headlight options were the same as DeSoto except the lights were recessed in body color pockets. Beautifully simple twin-tower taillights finished off the high-finned rear quarters. The license plate was set into a shadow box in the deck lid, a feature shared with DeSoto and Dodge as well. Side trim and paint treatments were very graphic. New Yorkers featured a full-length molding and slim color sweep together with seven identifying chrome louvres on the rear quarters. The revived Saratoga series (last offered in 1952) had a full-length body molding with a dart-shaped color panel optional on the rear fins. The low-line Windsors at first had no body moldings at all, but a three-quarter length version of the Saratoga molding was made optional midyear. A striking oval-shaped color panel was available on the rear quarters of all Windsors except the Town & Country wagon.

Originally Chrysler wagons were available only as six-passenger models, but a nine-passenger version with observation seat and Captive-Air tires was added in May. Engines included a Spitfire 354 cub-

*Even the bottom-of-the-line Chrysler Windsor was long, low and sleekly styled in 1957. It came standard with a 285-horsepower V8 and a three-speed manual transmission.*

The Saratoga represents the middle of the 1957 Chrysler line, while the New Yorker was Chrysler's best. The dart-shaped color molding on the Saratoga two-door hardtop (1) and four-door hardtop (2) was an option. The New Yorker (3, 4, 5) came with its molding and color insert standard. The seven chrome louvres were trademarks of the Chrysler New Yorker. There was a difference in muscle, too: Saratoga 295 horsepower; New Yorker 325 horsepower.

ic-inch V8 on Windsors, 285 hp; and Saratogas, 295 hp. New Yorkers were powered by the famous Firepower "hemi" with displacement of 392 cubic inches and 325 horsepower. Saratogas and New Yorkers both had four-barrel carburetors and dual exhausts.

Chrysler's 1957 model production (122,273) was actually some 6,000 units below that of 1956. Apparently, the new Imperial stole enough customers from the New Yorker to account for the decline.

## Imperial Styling

ADVERTISED AS "the finest expression of the Forward Look," the Imperial was just that. The graceful styling belied the fact that the car's wheelbase of 129 inches and overall length of 224 inches were reduced from 1956—the Imperial looked feet longer in spite of the reduced dimensions. The trademark gun-sight taillights were now positioned in the long, graceful fins. Between those outward-canted fins, the deck lid sloped gently to a twin-pod rear bumper. The sloping deck was available two ways: plain, with a simple center windsplit; or fancy, with a simulated rear tire cover inspired by Exner's K-310 show car. Both decks were set off with a large signature-style Imperial nameplate. The front end featured a delicate box-check grille; unfortunately, the distinctive split-grille theme used in 1955-56 was not continued. On single headlamp cars, the lights were con-

3

4

5

tained in massive finned cylinders and the optional dual headlights were placed in a simple large oval. Each design required its own unique grille endings. The front bumper was especially well executed, with wraparound twin horizontal blades reminiscent of the biplane bumpers of the 1934 Cadillac.

Roofs employed the first use of curved side glass in any American production car and all models featured a compound-curve windshield. The cars were now so low that the average person could look down on the roof. This created a new area for decorative treatment. Southamptons, or hardtops, sported a unique landau-style roof design in which the "C"- pillar molding swept up and over the roof in a graceful, peaked arch. The area behind the molding was body color, while the roof forward of

the molding was frequently a contrasting color.

There were three series: the Imperial, Imperial Crown, and the new Imperial LeBaron. The LeBaron name recalled Imperial's classic past. The LeBaron series was at first restricted to a four-door sedan, although a four-door hardtop was added midyear. LeBarons had a long list of standard equipment and their own exclusive wheel covers. The exteriors were available only in solid colors. Conservative, monotone broadcloth interiors were supplied in a time when two-tone upholstery was everywhere. The designers did get a bit carried away on the Imperial instrument panel, however, replacing the usual column-mounted turn signal lever with an inconvenient rocker switch located under the transmission pushbuttons.

The 300-C (1) was Chrysler's automotive bombshell. It was built specifically for performance and could be ordered with a 375- or 390-horsepower V8. The air scoops under the headlights helped cool the brakes. Only 484 such convertibles were built in '57. Imperial Crown (2 and 3) was as plush as the 300-C was gutsy. It was one of the first U.S. cars to have curved side-window glass, sharing the honor with Imperial and Imperial Le Baron.

# 1957 Chrysler/Imperial Specifications

| Make and Model | Dimensions | | | | Engines | | | | | Weight lbs. |
|---|---|---|---|---|---|---|---|---|---|---|
| | Wheelbase ins. | Overall Length ins. | Overall Width ins. | Overall Height ins. | 354 Cu. in. V8 285 Bhp | 354 cu. in. V8 295 Bhp | 392 cu. in. V8 325 Bhp | 292 cu. in. V8 375 Bhp | 392 cu. in. V8 390 Bhp | |
| Windsor | 126 | 219.2 | 78.8 | 57.8 | S | 0 | — | — | — | 3995 |
| Saratoga | 126 | 219.2 | 78.8 | 57.8 | — | S | — | — | — | 4165 |
| New Yorker | 126 | 219.2 | 78.8 | 57.9 | — | — | S | — | — | 4315 |
| 300-C | 126 | 219.2 | 78.8 | 57.9 | — | — | — | S | 0 | 4390 |
| Imperial | 129 | 224 | 81.2 | 56.7 | — | — | S | — | — | 4675 |

**Key:** *S: Standard Engine   O: Optional Engine*

Most exclusive of all the Imperials that year, but not built in America, was the Crown Imperial limousine. Stretched over a 149.5-inch wheelbase and handbuilt by Carrozzeria-Ghia of Torino, Italy, it went for over $12,000 a copy. The exclusive limousine (only 36 were built in 1957) was Chrysler's attempt to stay in the limousine business against Cadillac without spending a lot of money on production tooling. The handcrafted cars featured a special six-window roof with a black leather rear canopy and "Hy-Bridge" doors that opened into the roof for easier entry. Introduced in the summer of 1957, the Crown Imperial limousines used certain pull-ahead 1958 Imperial parts including grille, moldings, and other trim pieces.

## Big 300-C

THE BIG DADDY of the line was the mighty Chrysler 300-C, which auto writer Tom McCahill described

*Only 36 Imperial Crown Ghia Limousines were built in 1957. They were hand built in Italy and sold for over $12,000 each. Some of the trim pieces later appeared on '58 Imperials.*

as the "most hairy-chested, fire-eating land bomb ever conceived in Detroit . . . motorized dynamite." The 300-C, successor to the 1955 and 1956 NASCAR champion 300s, developed a whopping 375 horsepower at 5200 rpm. Special features included two four-barrel carbs, full race camshaft, mechanical lifters, adjustable valve rockers, heavy-duty crankshaft, double valve springs, tri-metal main and rod bearings, extra-deep exhaust valve seat inserts, and a "SilentFlite" fan which automatically cut out above 2500 rpm to boost power. There also was the "Optional Chassis Package" which included a 390 hp engine with a 10:1 compression ratio, longer duration high-speed cam, low back pressure exhaust system, limited slip differential, manual steering and manual transmission. Chrysler cautioned that "this optional engine is not recommended for the average 300-C customer . . ." which, of course, made the package all the more desirable. Thirteen different rear axle ratios were available on the 300, ranging from 2.92 to 6.17.

In testing the 300-C hardtop at Daytona, *Motor Trend* was amazed to find that not a single 0-60 mph run took more than 7.8 seconds, while the average 0-80 time was 12.6 seconds. Yet despite the increased performance, the magazine's testers reported that 300-C was a lot more tractable than previous 300s, with a softer ride and smoother-idling engine. The performance was still there, now made civilized.

A mammoth trapezoid grille and unique hood, lifted from Exner's "613" internal show car, dominated the front end. If you saw that in your rear view mirror, you moved over—quick. Other exclusive styling details included air scoops under the headlights (for brake cooling), special rear-quarter trim and genuine leather interiors. Only five colors were offered on 300s, and no two-tones. Almost 1200 two-door hardtops and 484 newly-introduced convertibles were built—double the 1956 production. These big macho cars were known everywhere as the "beautiful brutes."

# DESOTO

OF ALL EXNER finned fantasies, DeSotos (and Chryslers, which shared DeSoto sheet metal) were the cleanest models in Chrysler Corporation's 1957 lineup. The long, flowing rear quarters were especially smooth, ending in a handsome taillight assembly that consisted of three individual lights mounted in a chrome tower. These taillights were introduced in 1956 and were to remain a DeSoto trademark through 1959.

Side trim was a simple, straight moulding low on the body with a color sweep built off the molding standard on Fireflite Sportsman hardtops and convertible and optional on other models. Up front was an entirely original wide-mouth oval bumper set over a lower grille to give a look that was unique. Parking lights fitted into the outer ends of the upper bumper. Single or dual headlights were set into black painted, chrome-framed recesses in the front fenders on Fireflite and Firedome cars. The senior DeSotos were mounted over a 126-inch wheelbase and were powered by a 341 cubic-inch "hemi" V8. A two-barrel, 270-horsepower version was used on Firedomes, while Fireflites had a

four-barrel carburetor boosting horsepower to 295 hp. Dual exhausts were standard on convertibles only.

The big news at DeSoto was the new Firesweep series, a lower-priced line mounted on the Dodge 122-inch chassis. The car was an unusual combination of Dodge and DeSoto parts. Two- and four-door hardtops used Firedome roofs while the sedan and wagon used Dodge roofs and painted upper door frames. The front end combined the stock DeSoto bumper grille assembly with modified Dodge fenders, hood and cowl. Single headlights were nestled under a wide chrome lip that stretched across hood and fenders. The effect was somewhat bizarre but the Firesweep proved extremely popular, accounting for 35 percent of DeSoto production and winning *Car Life's* "Car of the Year" award in its class. Demand was so great that the Dodge main plant began turning out Firesweeps midyear. The small DeSotos were powered by the 325 cubic-inch Dodge V8 producing 245 horsepower; a power-pak option added another 15 horses. In addition, 100 Firesweep sedans

DeSoto Adventurer (1, 2, 3) was the flashy model in the DeSoto line, sporting plenty of gold trim. It came standard with a modified version of the engine found in the Fireflite (4). The engine produced one horsepower for every one of its 345 cubic inches.

▲ The four-door Fireflite Shopper (shown) and the four-door Fireflite Explorer were high-powered '57 DeSoto wagons.

Fireflite was the series in the regular DeSoto line for '57. Production hit 117,614 for the model year. ▼

## 1957 DeSoto Specifications

| Make and Model | Dimensions | | | | Engines | | | | | Weight lbs. |
|---|---|---|---|---|---|---|---|---|---|---|
| | Wheelbase ins. | Overall Length ins. | Overall Width ins. | Overall Height ins. | 325 cu. in. V8 245 Bhp | 325 cu. in. V8 260 Bhp. | 341 cu. in. V8 270 Bhp. | 341 cu. in. V8 295 Bhp | 345 cu. in. 345 Bhp | |
| Firesweep | 122 | 215.8 | 78.2 | 57 | S | 0 | — | — | — | 3675 |
| Firedome | 126 | 218 | 78.2 | 57 | — | — | S | — | — | 3955 |
| Fireflite | 126 | 218 | 78.2 | 57 | — | — | — | S | — | 4025 |
| Adventurer | 126 | 218 | 78.2 | 54 | — | — | — | — | S | 4025 |

**Key:** *S: Standard Engine   O: Optional Engine*

26

The DeSoto Firedome (1) and Fireflite (2) were basically set apart by trim, transmission and carburetion. The low-priced Firesweep (3) was a successful hodgepodge of Dodge and DeSoto parts. It held 35 percent of DeSoto sales.

equipped with Dodge six-cylinder engines were built, but these were not catalogued.

## DeSoto Adventurer

THE DESOTO Adventurer went the gold route with special gold anodized sunburst wheel covers, and gold-and-white as well as gold-and-black paint combinations were available. Special exterior treatment included five stainless steel trim strips on the deck lid and special "Adventurer" and checkered Forward Look ornaments on the rear quarters. There was also a custom interior. Unlike the Fury, however, the Adventurer came equipped with a special engine not available on other DeSotos. Basically a modified version of the Fireflite engine, the Adventurer mill had a "square" 3.80 by 3.80-inch bore and stroke, displacing 345 cubic inches and developing 345 hp—a highly desirable one horsepower per cubic inch. Engine modifications included heavier valve springs, special camshaft and intake manifold, and twin four-barrel carburetors. Torqueflite and power brakes were standard. Only 1560 two-door hardtops and 300 convertibles were assembled. A total of 117,614 DeSotos were produced in 1957 in what was to be DeSoto's last good year. Sales in '58 were less than half those of 1957 and the marque never recovered. It ceased production shortly following introduction of the 1961 models, after 33 years on the road.

# DODGE

THE DODGE was undoubtedly the gaudiest of all 1957 Exner creations, perhaps deliberately so. Dodges of the early 1950s were so dull that the division went overboard in 1955-57 trying to prove that Dodge was not the stick-in-the-mud car it had been for so long.

The saddle-type fin treatment lent itself to a variety of two-tone paint combinations. The customer could have the roof, fins, and lower body in one color and the hood, deck and upper body in a contrasting color; or just the roof and fins painted a contrasting color; or just the roof. Three-tone paint

1

combinations, a feature of the 1955-56 models, were thankfully absent.

The front end of the Dodge was very different, with a wide chrome molding flowing over the headlights and dipping between the fenders across the front. There was no conventional grille as such; instead, the grille consisted of a large chrome bar which dropped in the middle to enclose the Dodge crest. Split bumpers were used, each fitted with three small vertical guards on Custom Royal and Custom Sierra models. Wheelbase was 122 inches on all models: a two-inch increase over 1956.

Base engine on the Coronet Six was the same 230 cubic-inch L-head Six used in the Plymouth, but rated at six more horsepower. There were four versions of the 325 cubic-inch V8 beginning with the Red-Ram engine standard on Royal and Coronet series, developing 245 horsepower. Next was the Super Red-Ram V8 with a four-barrel carburetor, four-barrel intake manifold, special distributor, and dual exhausts rated at 260 hp. This engine was standard on Custom Royals and optional on other series. At the top of the line were two versions of the D-500 engine. These hot engines featured full hemispherical combustion chambers with dual rocker-shaft cylinder heads, 9.25:1 compression ratios, dual exhausts, and a four-barrel carburetor with matching intake manifolds. For real enthusiasts there was the Super D-500 engine with twin four-barrel carbs and 310 horsepower. The

Dodge Custom Royals were top-of-the-line models for 1957. The front end, as exhibited by the four-door sedan (1), had a horizontal chrome bar instead of a grille, and had a split front bumper. A side view of the Lancer two-door hardtop (2) shows the model's distinctive trim. That trim also appeared on four-door Custom Royals (3), which had the same 122-inch wheelbase as the two-door Custom Royal Lancer models.

| ▲ The dual stacked taillights shown on the Dodge Coronet Lancer Convertible were carried on from previous years. | The Coronet series, including the four-door sedan, ▼ was available in a six-cylinder and V8 version. |

only clue to all this power was a discreet D-500 emblem on the deck lid.

## Options Offered

THERE WERE no special Dodge offerings in 1957, but Texas dealers could order special "Texan" emblems on Coronets (except the convertible) installed on rear quarters, deck lid, and glovebox door for $10.50.

An interesting option offered on Dodge and other corporation cars was the "Highway Hi-Fi" record

The Dodge Custom Sierra station wagon for 1957 (1) was available only in a four-door version. It could be ordered with either two or three seats. Dodge was first to offer a rear-facing third seat. Of the Dodge Royal Lancers, the two-door (2) was the most in demand. The Royal Lancer two-door cost about $3000.

## 1957 Dodge Specifications

| Make and Model | Dimensions | | | | Engines | | | | | | | | | Weight lbs. |
|---|---|---|---|---|---|---|---|---|---|---|---|---|---|---|
| | Wheelbase ins. | Overall Length ins. | Overall Width ins. | Overall Height ins. | 230 cu. in. Six 138 Bhp | 325 cu. in. V8 245 Bhp. | 325 cu. in. V8 320 Bhp. | 325 cu. in. V8 260 Bhp | 325 cu. in. V8 235 Bhp. | 325 cu. in. V8 285 Bhp. | 325 cu. in. V8 345 Bhp | 325 cu. in. V8 310 Bhp. | 325 cu. in. V8 350 Bhp. | |
| Coronet Six | 122 | 212.2 | 77.9 | 56.6 | S | | | | | | | | | 3470 |
| Coronet V8 | 122 | 212.2 | 77.9 | 56.6 | — | S | 0 | 0 | 0 | 0 | 0 | 0 | 0 | 3620 |
| Coronet Royal | 122 | 212.2 | 77.9 | 56.6 | — | S | 0 | 0 | 0 | 0 | 0 | 0 | 0 | 3620 |
| Custom Royal | 122 | 212.2 | 77.9 | 56.8 | — | — | — | S | 0 | 0 | 0 | 0 | 0 | 3690 |
| D-500 (Engine Option) | 122 | 212.2 | 77.9 | 56.6 | — | — | — | — | — | S | 0 | 0 | 0 | 3690 |

**Key:** *S: Standard Engine  O: Optional Engine*

player, first introduced in 1956. This compact record player used specially designed 16-2/3 rpm records which played up to 60 minutes on each side. The unit, insulated so the needle would not slip on rough roads, was mounted beneath the center of the instrument panel.

Even the trucks received the fin treatment as Dodge introduced the Sweptside 100 pickup in May, 1957. The truck used Dodge two-door station wagon rear quarters and taillights mounted flush with the front cab to give Dodge an answer to Ford's new Ranchero.

# PLYMOUTH

NEW AS THE new 1957 Plymouth was, it was actually a logical development of previous styling themes. The abrupt fins were takeoffs on the '56 model, while the tall triangular taillights were exaggerated versions of those introduced in 1954. The sharply undercut, "catch me—I'm falling" fender first appeared in 1955, as did the crease feature on the rear quarter panel and the recessed cove under the deck lid. Plymouth managed to be both evolutionary and revolutionary at the same time.

Wheelbase was increased from 115 to 118 inches on all but the wagons, which went to a 122-inch wheelbase. The front end for the first time made use of a separate stone pan below a bilevel bumper whose raised center section was said to eliminate the need for add-on guards. The horizontal bar grille above the bumper carried Plymouth's last

The double side-trim strips, sometimes with a color panel, were standard on Belvederes such as the two-door hardtop (1) and convertible (2). The Belvedere instrument panel included pushbuttons on the extreme left of the dash that controlled the optional three-speed TorqueFlite automatic transmission. Defroster airflow could be adjusted by turning the vents positioned on either side of the dashboard-mounted mirror. Options included a record player situated under the center of the instrument panel.

version of its traditional sailing ship ornament, while the stone pan below the bumper featured six large vertical cooling slots beneath the center section. There was some customer objection to the size of the slots, however, and by January a vertical bar had been added to each of the slots to make them less noticeable. Midyear also saw the addition of a Savoy four-door hardtop.

Side trim was simple and effective. On Belvedere and Sport Suburban models, a slim and bright molding ran front to rear with an additional molding below to form a tapered color sweep if desired. Savoys and Custom Suburbans used a single horizontal molding from the front door to the rear bumper, which was made into a two-tone area by the addition of a diagonal molding on the door. This treatment was optional on Plaza and Deluxe Suburbans as well. Accessory "coolie hat" wheel covers became instant favorites among customizers.

## Engine Choices

ENGINES INCLUDED a 230 cubic-inch, 132 horsepower Powerflow Six, available on all but the convertible; a Hy-Fire 277 cubic-inch, 197 hp V8 available only on Plazas; a Fury 301 cubic-inch, 215 hp V8 standard on Belvedere, Savoy, and Suburban V8 models; and the Fury 301 with power-pak that boosted horsepower to 235. Biggest bomb was the Fury V-800 engine, a 318 cubic-inch V8 developing 290 hp. This engine, with its 9.25:1 compression ratio, featured an eight-barrel carburetion system with balanced fuel flow to each cylinder and separate idle air-bleed inlets; matching intake manifold; two special offset air cleaners; special pistons; high-performance cam and spark plugs; and a low-restriction, dual-exhaust system. This engine was optional in all models, including the lightweight Plaza business coupe. Lest there be a mistake about the intent of this option, a famous ad

2

| ▲ Lower molding and color panel were standard on Plymouth's Savoys, optional on Plaza and Deluxe Suburban models. | The 1957 Plymouth Fury was available only as an eggshell white, two-door hardtop with a special V-800 ▼ engine. |

showed a driver behind the wheel of what was obviously a '57 Chevy coming up behind a V-800 Plymouth on the drag strip. The caption read, "It's no use buddy—that's a Plymouth with a Fury V-800." Others ads showed the proud Plymouth drivers being congratulated by friends while Ford and Chevy drivers sulked against their cars in the background.

The Fury was essentially a specially trimmed two-door hardtop equipped with the same V-800 engine and heavy-duty chassis that was available on lesser Plymouths. Available only in eggshell white, the Fury used specially designed gold anodized aluminum side trim and gold upper grille

# 1957 Plymouth Specifications

| Make and Model | Dimensions | | | | Engines | | | | | Weight lbs. |
|---|---|---|---|---|---|---|---|---|---|---|
| | Wheelbase ins. | Overall Length ins. | Overall Width ins. | Overall Height ins. | 230 cu.in. 6-cyl. 132 Bhp. | 318 cu. in. V8 290 Bhp. | 301 cu. in. V8 215 Bhp. | 301 cu. in. V8 235 Bhp. | 277 cu. in. V8 197 Bhp. | |
| Plaza | 118 | 204.6 | 78.2 | 56.2 | 0 | 0* | — | 0 | S | 3405 |
| Savoy | 118 | 204.6 | 78.2 | 56.5 | 0 | 0* | S | 0 | — | 3475 |
| Belvedere | 118 | 204.6 | 78.2 | 56.5 | 0 | 0* | S | 0 | — | 3475 |
| Fury | 118 | 204.6 | 78.2 | 53 | — | S | — | — | — | 3475 |
| Suburban | 122 | 204.6 | 78.2 | 56.5 | 0 | 0* | S | 0 | — | 3475 |

**Key:** *S: Standard Engine  O: Optional Engine*

*Belvedere four-door featured Plymouth's below-bumper cooling slots. They brought consumer disapproval.*

bars, special wheel covers and front fender ornaments, custom instrument panel cluster, and a custom interior. Just 7438 were built.

*Hot Rod* magazine tested a Torqueflite-equipped Belvedere hardtop with a power-pak Fury 301 V8 against the Fury equipped with the standard three-speed synchromesh transmission. The Belvedere averaged 9.6 seconds 0-60 mph while the Fury did somewhat better at 8.6 seconds, but neither car was the fastest that *Hot Rod* had tested. The magazine noted that the Belvedere could outdrag the Fury for the first 100 feet or more, a situation attributed generally to the superiority of the Torqueflite transmission over the stock shifter.

# GENERAL MOTORS CORPORATION

**T**O SAY that General Motors was the most formidable automotive colossus in 1957 is as unnecessary as saying the same of it in 1980, but it is nevertheless as true of one year as of the other. GM recorded net sales 23 years ago of close to $11 billion and income of $844 million, retaining $275 million of that for use in improving the business. In 1976, the figures were $47 billion, $2 billion and $1.3 billion respectively; but the world and GM have grown considerably in the meantime.

In the passenger-car business, only one—although the most important—of GM's broad interests, Chevrolet Division, was destined in 1957 to lose its time-honored top sales position to Ford. But this was only temporary. In the midst of Chevy's slump, GM built close to three million cars and had four makes among the top six. Several of its single models were produced in greater quantity than the entire output of American Motors Corporation and Studebaker-Packard combined.

GM's upper management was populated with greats, a veritable New York Yankees of Fifties autodom: President Harlow Curtice, raised in the tradition of Alfred Sloan; design chief Harley Earl, six-foot-three, a giant both physically and professionally, the father of automotive styling; Chevrolet Division General Manager Ed Cole, a peerless engineer; Pontiac General Manager Semon E. "Bunky" Knudsen; Cadillac's James M. Roche. Two of the last three were destined to be GM presidents in later years, with their company riding a 50 percent market share and moving toward 60 percent.

Ed Cole symbolized the men who put GM where it was. Only 46 years old in 1957, he was already well on his way toward the presidency (which he would achieve as the youngest man to hold the job). Cole had worked his way up from the ranks, graduating from the GM Institute in the early 1930s. He was a major contributor to Cadillac's modern overhead-valve V8 in 1949, creator of the compact Cadet after the war, and the man behind Chevrolet's superb 265 V8 of 1955. The latter was begun about a day after Cole had arrived at Chevrolet in 1952. A rather heavy 230 cubic-inch unit had been planned, but Cole scrapped it and had the 265 running within six months—weighing less than the old stovebolt six.

Cole, the engineer's engineer, set stringent standards. "An engine must be made to hang together under any circumstances," he often said. He summed up a widespread GM company attitude this way: "Nothing is more important than product. We must always have an outstanding product. That is my first interest. With a good product, the sales force is automatically inspired to set new records."

**New Tech Center**

THE MOST celebrated news at the outset of 1957 was GM's new technical center at Warren, Michigan. Sprawling over 320 acres, it was home for what Harlow Curtice called "the inquiring mind." Staffed with 4700 scientists, engineers, designers and technicians who hardly began to fill the place, it was planned for massive enlargement.

Architecturally the Tech Center lived up to the activities it housed. It was a beautiful structure that even today looks modern, in a manicured park with 22-acre lake. Typical of the broadness of approach was the ornamental fountain, pumping 166 bathtubs worth of water every minute.

The Tech Center housed five of what GM called "staffs." In order of seniority, they were: Research, Engineering, Styling, Process Development and Service—the latter being for internal administration. Naturally, the Tech Center embraced many products besides cars. Early activities produced a silent butler that cleaned dishes by ultrasonic waves and a bank of six free-piston engines to

Cadillac's Eldorado Biarritz featured a new-style sloping deck and reshaped fins.

power a new cargo ship. The automotive teams who first arrived there worked on new lines for 1959 and beyond, while finishing the 1958s.

The GM automotive lineup for 1957 was a mixture of all-new and drastically facelifted models. At the top end of the line, the "B" and "C" body cars of Cadillac, Buick, and Oldsmobile were completely redesigned. The "A" body Chevrolets and Pontiacs made do with facelifts—drastic ones, to be sure; both faced all-new rivals from Ford and Plymouth, Mercury, Dodge, and DeSoto. Chevrolet, in turn, spent over $200 million to retool for 1957.

GM engineering saw fuel injection being readied for use in several cars; a greatly expanded line of station wagons, featuring for the first time four-door hardtop wagons; the new, ultraluxurious Cadillac Eldorado Brougham; and the now well-established fiberglass Corvette, already in its fourth year as America's first (or at least only surviving) postwar sports car.

## Hopes for Rebound

GM HAD SCORED big in banner 1955, taken a major production cut in 1956, and was hoping to rebound in 1957. Harlow Curtice felt that 1956 sales had fallen off due to the "great deal of publicity at the beginning of the year [which] had continued to some extent, about the revolutionary models that would be available in 1957, and that they would be introduced early by comparison with 1956." In fact, the '57s arrived at the usual time, and a lot of promised advances—fuel injection, supercharging,

air suspension, torsion bars—either did not work or were exotic, high-priced options.

GM entered 1957 with its usual group of three bodyshells for five makes. A common alteration to most of its cars was the switch to 14-inch wheels. This was mainly a styling gimmick, although they were also said to improve ride. GM had planned dual headlights for 1957, but eight states delayed passing laws to accommodate them, and "quadralights" were held up until 1958. The Eldorado Brougham had them, mainly because it was introduced later than other cars and after more states had passed the needed legislation.

General Motors managed to avoid some fads such as pushbutton transmissions and towering tailfins, while introducing certain fetishes of its own: huge windshields with reverse-angle vent panes, and three-window backlights. Overall, GM styling was improved over 1956, with certain garish exceptions. There was no sign yet of a check in the growth of car size, although as Volkswagen sales multiplied in late 1957, GM began shipping 1000 Vauxhalls and 1000 Opels a month from England and Germany respectively to its Buick and Pontiac dealers. Back at the Tech Center, plans began to gel for GM's own compact, with rear-mounted, air-cooled engine—another contribution of Ed Cole.

Absent in 1957 for the first time in five years was that annual orgy of PR pomp, the Motorama. Beginning in 1949 and repeating in 1950 and 1953-56, these expensive galas attracted a combined ten million people to road shows ranging from Boston to Miami to San Francisco. They traditionally featured the new production cars from each division, plus enough wild experimentals and one-offs to stir the blood of any car lover.

GM temporarily abandoned the Motorama in 1957, possibly because it had enough momentum built up from the past four. The attractive Nomad hardtop wagon had debuted as a Corvette model at the '54 show, for example, and was in production on a wagon chassis by 1955. Oldsmobile's Delta, from the 1956 show, predicted the shape of GM cars in 1957 and 1958. The Eldorado Brougham of 1957 could trace its heritage to Motorama show cars as early as 1953. The overall styling feature of dropped beltlines, identifying GM cars from One-Fifty Chevy to Eldorado Seville, began with the Motorama show cars of the early '50s.

The Motoramas returned in 1959 and 1961, but on a much smaller scale. After that they disappeared for good; they were victims of TV and the need for privacy by GM designers. One former executive said, "The competition was ripping off everything GM did."

### Chevy Race Car

ONE SPECIAL that did make news in 1957 was the Chevy Super Sports, which appeared at Florida's Sebring road course in March. Ostensibly a Corvette, it was completely unlike the Chevy sports car, although it ran the 283 cubic-inch V8 (much modified). The SS was built around a space frame, with a magnesium body and wheels. It featured De Dion rear suspension and inboard brakes, and weighed 1000 pounds less than a production Corvette.

In the hands of both Juan Fangio and Stirling Moss, the SS broke the Sebring lap record, causing one writer to call it "America's first serious road car since the Stutz DV32." Chevy insiders said it might cost $6000 to build the SS in limited quantity. Some of them hoped it would challenge the racing Maseratis and Ferraris as an all-American champion.

Unfortunately, the Automobile Manufacturers Association, including GM, unanimously recommended in May that factories not engage in or encourage the use of their cars in racing. The recommendation was the result of an antiracing campaign by the National Safety Council and others who insisted that the sport did not improve the breed.

So General Motors never fielded a sports racing car to do battle with Europe's greats in 1957. What it did produce were some of the best-styled cars in its postwar history as well as—with Chevrolet—one of its most clever facelifts. In the process, it fulfilled an old Al Sloan dictum: "A car for every purse and pocket."

# BUICK

IN 1957, BUICK lost the third place position in the production race that it had wrested from Plymouth in 1954 for the first time since 1930. The 25 percent drop in production probably can be attributed more to fine new designs from Buick rivals in the highly competitive mid-price field, rather than to any fault of Buick itself. The cars from Flint, Michigan, were entirely redesigned for 1957, as were the Cadillacs. The improvement was considerable.

Exactly what the cost of the restyling was, Buick General Manager Ed Ragsdale never said. It must have run into several hundred million, though, because it was the most sweeping alteration since the prewar cars of 1948 changed to the first all-postwar Buicks of 1949. The cars were garish, but that was in vogue in 1957; Buick merely fitted its styling to the times. It should have been a much more successful year than it was. Virgil Exner's Chrysler

products may have been the real culprits. If so, their effect belies the theory that in 1957 cars had to look like juke boxes to sell.

Mechanically, the line of Specials, Centurys, Supers and Roadmasters retained Buick's ageless torque tube drive and coil spring suspension on all four wheels. Strictly by Ragsdale's choice, the 15-inch wheel was held over despite an industry-wide trend to 14-inchers. "We see absolutely no advantage whatsoever in the 14-inch wheel," Ragsdale said. "We personally like the appearance of the 15-inch wheel in relation to the size of the car."

The Buick engine was greatly enlarged, from 322 cubic-inches to 364, and on the upper models it produced 300 horsepower. This was especially significant for the Century: with its smaller and lighter "B" body, it remained the hottest Buick of all, as it had been for some years. In the transmission de-

Buick Super models such as the Super four-door Riviera had the same 127.5-inch wheelbase as Roadmasters. The cars measured 215.3 inches overall and were 77.6 inches wide.

partment, Dyna-flow Drive was standard on all models except the Special, which came with three-speed stick unless Dyna-flow was specified (at $220 extra). Manual Specials also used 8:1 compression, against 9.5:1 with automatic. A new Dyna-flow feature in 1957 was "Variable Pitch," which Buick said brought performance "to a new high with absolute smoothness in any speed range from start to cruising." The idea really stemmed from a need to make transmissions last longer. The driver could now change the pitch of the stator blade for maximum performance in the "drive" range, by depressing the accelerator fully to the floor.

### Longer and Lower

THE NEW BUICKS were longer by about three inches, lower, but—surprisingly—not wider. In fact, they were about one inch narrower. The only wheelbase change was the half inch added to Super and Roadmaster models. A brand new model range was the Roadmaster Series 75. It comprised a pair of hardtops, four doors or two, fitted with a full line of accessories including leather or fabric custom interior, dual exhausts, flexible spoke steering wheel, speed reminder, Dyna-flow, power steering and power brakes.

Another new model in the Special and Century lines was the "Caballero" station wagon, with four-door hardtop styling and a deluxe interior inspired by the Chevrolet Nomad and Pontiac Safari, two nice-looking wagons with hardtoplike styling that were first introduced in 1955. Buick increased wagon production threefold to meet expected demand, and Flint production lines were now turning out wagon bodies themselves. Prior to 1957, Buick had the Mitchell Bentley Corp. hack its wagon bodies out of sedans, with resultant supply

problems and limited production.

Buick spent much time and money on its 1957 interiors. Like the Cadillac's, the Buick's instrument panel was all new and nodded to safety with recessed knobs and standard padding. The speedometer needle was replaced by a series of red segments that popped up suddenly at five mile per hour increments. Buick panels retained needle instruments for amperes and oil pressure as well as fuel and temperature, and the top of the panel was removable to get at them. The glove compartment was moved close to the driver (but not quite centralized), and all minor controls were grouped under the instrument panel.

Although he had switched to ball-joint front suspension for '57, Buick Chief Engineer Vern Mathews pointed to big advantages in his retention of coil springs and torque tube drive. They were: a

## 1957 Buick Division Specifications

| Make and Model | Dimensions | | | | Engines | | Weight lbs. |
| | Wheelbase ins. | Overall Length ins. | Overall Width ins. | Overall Height ins. | 364 cu. in. V8 250 Bhp | 364 cu. in. V8 300 Bhp. | |
|---|---|---|---|---|---|---|---|
| 40 Special | 122 | 208.4 | 74.9 | 58 | S | — | 3956 |
| 60 Century | 122 | 208.4 | 74.9 | 59 | — | S | 4156 |
| 50 Super | 127.5 | 215.3 | 77.6 | 59 | — | S | 4359 |
| 70 Roadmaster | 127.5 | 215.3 | 77.6 | 59 | — | S | 4469 |

**Key:** S: Standard Engine   O: Optional Engine

| ▲ Of a total 405,086 Buicks built in 1957, only 4085 Buick Century Convertibles came off the assembly line. | One of the models that maintained popularity despite a bad year for Buick was the 1957 Roadmaster ▼ Convertible. |
|---|---|

sealed drive train, easier matching of front and rear spring frequencies, and the fact that rear springs were not tied to engine power because the axle was fixed in relation to the driveshaft. Leaf springs, in contrast, had to absorb acceleration and braking forces. The result of all this, testers said, was a marshmallow ride and dangerously sloppy handling. It has been suggested by the author of one recent book that this did not matter, because the average motorist does not drive like a car critic around a test track. The fact is that the average person could easily get into a situation where fast maneuvering is the only way to avoid an accident. In such a case, he would be almost as unsafe as possible in the 1957 Buick. Meanwhile, certain Buicks packed enough performance to easily get a

Flash was the theme of the '57 Buick's styling, as displayed by the extended rear chrome gravel shields and wraparound front bumper of the Century two-door hardtop (1). The Caballero was a new Century hardtop wagon introduced in 1957 (2). Buick's Special two-door hardtop was its best-selling model (3).

driver in just that sort of situation. The Century, for example, could leap the standing quarter mile in just 17.6 seconds at 81 mph and reel off 0-60 mph in nine seconds and 0-80 in 15.

## Few Other Changes

UP AND DOWN the Buick line, with the exception of the Caballero wagons and new Roadmaster 75s, the basic lineup remained approximately the same as 1956. The Series 40 Special came in at $2596 for the two-door sedan. That was a competitive price, but over $200 more than the same model had cost the year before. Specials were offered in two- and four-door sedans and hardtops, plus two varieties of "Estate Wagons."

*The Buick Century Riviera Coupe came standard with Buick's 300-horsepower V8 engine.*

The Buick Century could not be had for less than $3234 in 1957 (again, some $200 over 1956), and most models listed for around $4000 ex-showroom. The Century was available as a four-door sedan, two- and four-door hardtops, an Estate Wagon and a two-door convertible. The Super came only in hardtops and convertibles, while the hefty Roadmaster was priced just short of Cadillac with a wider variety of the same body styles. Power steering was optional on Specials and Centurys at $107 extra, and air conditioning could be had on any model if one could pay the $430 price. Air conditioning was still in its infancy, and not cheap.

There is probably less collector interest in the 1957 Buick than all the GM marques with the possible exception of Oldsmobile. It is, of course, only 20 years old, and for the hobbyist it is only just beginning to come into range as a possible candidate for the old car concours circuit. Undoubtedly the luxurious Roadmaster 75 is the model to find, although it is not common. A real sleeper is the speedy Century, a well-known road car in its day and one of the fastest full-size GM cars of the Fifties. On the whole, collector interest in Buicks remains centered on the earlier straight Eights, drifting over toward the Skylarks of 1953-54, then skipping ahead to the razor-edge Rivieras of 1963-65.

# CADILLAC

THE YEAR 1957 was an important one for Cadillac styling: it was perhaps the first year since 1949 that Cadillacs exhibited really first-rate design. The cars were lower and cleaner looking from nearly every angle. The thin, clean look was achieved through styling rather than body configuration; but the overall height of the cars had nevertheless been reduced by three inches in sedans and two inches in coupes.

The shorter stature was achieved through the use of a new X-frame, formed by two girders welded together at the center. Viewed from above, the frame resembled an hourglass. It left little protection against broadside collisions because the frame rails between front and rear wheels were elimi-

nated, but Cadillac compensated for this by strengthening the rocker panels.

With this new frame, the styling staff brushed aside the heretofore bulky look of Cadillacs, applying less-prominent grillework and a wider, more rakish windshield with reverse-angled vent panes. Still prominent were the "Dagmar" front bumper guards, which were the subject of many pointed complaints and guffaws by the press. One editor, for example, thought they were fine for the Cadillac but hellish on anything they tapped. He said, "True, they have rubber tips, but they still amount to the most lethal pair of nursing bottles the poor young Chevrolet in a parking lot can ever encounter."

The rest of the 1957 restyle was a big improve-

*Series 62 models were the least expensive of all 1957 Cadillac cars. The four-door weighed about 4600 pounds and had a 130-inch wheelbase. Base engine was a 300-hp V8.*

ment. The abrupt, upright tailfin-taillights of 1948-56, which had been growing taller since their introduction, were gone. New round units were positioned at mid-fender and set into modest housings. The fenders themselves, although finned, were not huge. The dipped beltline that was a mark of Harley Earl styling since 1953 was still there, but the vertical chrome trim that had formed a simulated scoop on the 1956 Cadillac was gone. In fact, the only side embellishment was an unobtrusive bullet-shaped applique on the rear fenders and a less-imposing fake scoop running underneath.

### Eldorado Styling

THE LIMITED-PRODUCTION Cadillac Eldorado continued to forecast future styling features of the main line. For example, in 1957 the Cadillac goddess hood ornament was replaced by the twin fins the Eldorado had used in 1956; the 1957 Eldorado, again predicting things to come, wore no hood ornament at all. (The large, sculpted goddess of 1941 was still optional on all models.) The '57 Eldo also predicted future tail ends, with its sharply canted, inboard-mounted fins topping round, rear-tapered fenders. Eldorados continued to sport "sabre spoke" wheel covers. The Seville coupe used cloth covering over its metal roof. Other low-production Cadillacs included the Fleetwood cars, Series 75 and 60 Special—the latter being the first pillarless 60 Special in Cadillac history.

The instrument panel also was redesigned in 1957, and the result was generally considered an improvement over previous units. All controls were

*Like other 1957 Cadillacs, the Coupe DeVille was three inches lower than 1956 models.*

Cadillac's Series 60 Sedan (1) became a hardtop in '57 and was set apart from other models by its wide, rear chrome panel. Clean lines and rubber-cushioned "bullet" bumper tips set off the Eldorado Biarritz (2). It represented a totally new body style from the previous year. The Eldorado Seville (4) was the hardtop version, priced at about $7300. At 236 inches, the Series 75 Limousine (3) was a foot longer than the Series 60 Sedan.

3

clearly labeled and lighted at night—even to the hidden cigar lighters, buried in the ashtrays. Following a current fad, the glovebox was moved to a central position where it was more convenient to the driver. Features appeared that are with us today: the parking brake foot pedal, and air conditioning units that were taken out of the rear package shelf and mounted up front on the dash.

## Mark II Rival

A RIVAL to Ford Motor Company's Continental Mark II was the new Eldorado Brougham, a glittering dream car come true. Priced at a towering $13,074, about $3000 more than the Mark II, it was

introduced at the New York Automobile Show December 8, 1956. Brougham styling was fostered mainly by Harley Earl, and had antecedants in Earl's Motorama show cars. The four-door hardtop Cadillac Orleans of 1953 had contributed the Brougham's pillarless body construction, with front doors front-hinged and rear doors rear-hinged; the 1954 Park Avenue had suggested its brushed stainless steel roof; and the 1955 Eldorado Brougham Town Car closely projected its styling.

Broughams came as standard with most usual accessories, plus several that were entirely their own. Base price included air conditioning; power seat (with a memory that adjusted it automatically to a preset position no matter how it had been

2

moved); power brakes, steering, windows, vent wings, door locks and trunk lid; air suspension; Hydra-matic transmission; complete instrumentation; and radio with automatic-disappearing antenna. Special Brougham equipment included Arpege perfume in an atomizer, stored neatly in a makeup mirror in a rear armrest; grey-tinted glass in all windows and polarized sun visors that became darker or lighter according to the degree of tilt; a set of six silver magnetized tumblers for the glove box; cigarette case; tissue dispenser; lipstick and stick cologne.

Brougham styling was admittedly on the gaudy side, in brash contrast to the conservative Continental. Yet, the overall effect was good, and the

Brougham actually looked like a compact Cadillac. Its performance was reasonable, with 60 miles per hour attained in 13 seconds from rest and a top speed of near 110 mph. Production was intentionally limited, so the car was not for everyone. GM later admitted the whole exercise had been designed strictly to outdo the Mark II, and that the corporation had lost about $10,000 on every Brougham sold.

### Air Bag Suspension

THE ELDO BROUGHAM'S suspension system was a controversial affair, purportedly designed to provide a perfect ride regardless of vehicle load or

*The luxurious 1957 Eldorado Brougham, available only as a four-door hardtop, had self-leveling air suspension, Mouton rugs, and a full range of other extravagant features.*

road surface. Instead of springs, it used four rubber airbags at each wheel with each bag having its own rubber diaphragm and piston. An air compressor and accumulator, air piping, leveling valves, and solenoid controls were designed to hold a constant axle clearance and keep the ride absolutely level. The system was optional on other Cadillacs whose suspensions were designed to accept either air bags or standard coil springs.

Cadillac's air suspension differed from the optional units of other GM cars in that it used an open-type air system. The engine air cleaner supplied air to the compressor; it exhausted to the outside atmosphere. Cadillac's system also used a yoke instead of the upper two rear links. A manual control under the dash was used by the driver to fully pressurize the air bags when negotiating rutted roads or a steep driveway.

The problem with Cadillac and other air suspensions was that the ride improvement was not justified by the cost or complexity. The units were difficult and expensive to service, and given to blowing out at embarrassing moments. Today a deflated air bag is even more trouble to the Brougham owner, because spare parts are so much more scarce. Many Broughams were converted to coil spring suspension after 1957, and relatively few originals still function as they were intended to. Brougham aficionados with original cars consider them superior in ride, particularly at cruising speeds. But Brougham owners admit that it takes a technician to keep the car running right.

For collectors, the Eldorado Brougham is the most desirable 1957 Cadillac, although scarce: only 704 were built during 1957-58. More Broughams were made in Italy through 1960, but they lacked the exceptional standards of finish and equipment. Eldorados, of course, are collectible; but other 1957 Cadillacs have generally not reached that stage. It is difficult to understand why, because 1957 represented a high point in postwar Cadillac design. In 1958 the styling went garish again, and it didn't begin to recover until the mid-Sixties.

## 1957 Cadillac Division Specifications

| Make and Model | Dimensions | | | | Engines | | Weight lbs. |
| | Wheelbase ins. | Overall Length ins. | Overall Width ins. | Overall Height ins. | 365 cu. in. V8 300 Bhp. | 365 cu. in. V8 325 Bhp.* | |
|---|---|---|---|---|---|---|---|
| Series 62 | 130 | 215.9 | 80 | 59.1 | S | 0 | 4595 |
| Series 60 Special | 133 | 224.4 | 80 | 59.1 | S | 0 | 4600 |
| Series 75 | 150 | 236 | 80 | 61.6 | S | 0 | 4600 |
| Eldorado | 129.5 | 222.1 | 80 | 58.4 | S | 0 | 4620 |

*Standard engine on air conditioned models

**Key:** *S: Standard Engine  O: Optional Engine*

# CHEVROLET

EDWARD NICHOLAS Cole, general manager of Chevrolet in 1957 and father of its V8 engine, was asked at new model time how he assessed the challenge from Ford. The Dearborn rival, reporters told Cole, had fully redesigned for '57, and was "coming out swinging" with its new line against a three-year-old facelift at Chevrolet.

Cole's reply was typical of Chevy's energetic, confident leader: "You've got to get up off the canvas before you start swinging." After all, Ford had ended 1956 a quarter million vehicles behind Chevrolet.

A fight for production supremacy had raged between the two makes since 1954, with Ford coming close but never quite delivering the knockout punch to Chevrolet. In 1955 it was nearly a tie, but Chevy pulled away again in 1956. In 1957, Ford felt, victory was at hand.

Chevrolet faced 1957 with a dated body, but the division was still confident that the body was a good one. Today, 1955-57 Chevrolets are the most popular models in the firm's history—possibly the most popular postwar passenger cars of all—with a 7000-member national owners club and 3000 more enthusiasts dedicated to the Chevy Nomad wagon. The 1955-57s popularity has been consistent.

Styling in '57 was an excellent facelift of the good-looking 1955 body, featuring neat rear tailfins that added definition to the stern quarters. The front end, interior and dashboard were completely altered, although the clean 1955-56 grilles were succeeded by an expensive oval bumper/grille housing gold or silver mesh and a broad horizontal bar containing the Chevy emblem and parking lights. Twin windsplits broke up the old hood line, but served no other function. The hooded headlights were surrounded by meshed openings for fresh air, which was ducted through the fenders and into the passenger compartment. This allowed rust-beset fenders to remain relatively dry through ram effect. A stainless steel applique, in the shape of a forward-tapering triangle, distinguished the top-line Bel Air's rear fenders. This area was painted on the midrange Two-Ten and absent on the One-Fifty. Stylists had managed to increase the glass area from 69 to 75 square inches, and to offer 460 model and color combinations—96 more than in 1956. There were 17 exterior colors comprising 16 solids and 15 two-tones.

**Chevy Performance**

"IT WILL take more than styling to sell cars," Ed Cole said about his 1957 Chevy. If sales records are

*In 1957, Corvette got a power boost from a 283-horsepower, fuel-injected V8.*

any guide, he was quite right. Performance was the name of the game in the low-priced field: Plymouth's hot Fury was in its second year and Ford was fielding engines of up to 300 horsepower. Chevy, which had benefited from Cole's V8s since 1955, was not left behind. Its 1957 story was summed up in its leading advertising slogan, "One horsepower for every cubic inch." It ended the year a shade behind Ford, but still sold 1.5 million cars.

The 283 cubic-inch V8 was achieved by boring the 265-inch engine 1/8 inch and raising power through higher compression, higher lift cams and four-barrel carburetors, dual Fours or fuel injection. The latter induction system, with 10.5 compression, resulted in the 283 hp 283 cubic-inch figure. Engine refinements in 1957 also included full pressure (instead of metered to valve lifters) lubrication, mechanical lifters in fuel injected engines, increased top deck thickness in the V8 block (to minimize cylinder wall distortion through overtight head bolts), longer-reach spark plugs, and increased cross-sectional gas passage areas in the

inlet ports and exhaust manifolds (for better scavenging and improved volumetric efficiency). The Chevy Six, meanwhile, was unchanged, still developing 140 horsepower.

GM-designed fuel injection consisted of fuel and air meters and a manifold assembly. It supplied an exact air/fuel mixture to each intake port. Taking bows with FI in '57 was the new three-speed Turboglide automatic, available only with the 283 V8s. Turboglide used three turbines, two planetary gear sets, and a variable-pitch stator and torque converter in an aluminum housing; it weighed 82 pounds less than Powerglide. It converted engine power to motion by rotating oil in the torque converter in the three turbines, which rotated depending on their vane positions and the speeds desired. The turbines took over from one another imperceptibly, without the "lurch" of Powerglide. Turbo quadrants contained an Hr position, which stood for "Hill Retarder." Designed to provide braking when descending hills, it created a turbulence in the oil of the torque converter.

The 283 V8 (1) in 185- and 283-horsepower versions was an option in the Bel Air line, Chevy's top series in 1957. The Bel Air was distinguished from the Two-Ten by its aluminum side trim panel, decorative front fender louvres and chrome rocker panels. The Bel Air line included a six-passenger four-door wagon (2), a four-door sedan (3), a two-door hardtop (4), a convertible (5) and a two-door Nomad wagon (6), plus a two-door sedan and four-door hardtop.

1

*Chevrolet's middle-of-the-line
series was the Two-Ten. The
series included a four-door
sedan (1), four-door hardtop (2),
two-door, six-passenger Handyman
station wagon (3), two-door
hardtop (4), four-door nine-
passenger Beauville wagon (5),
plus a two-door sedan. Standard
drive train included a 235 cubic-
inch Six developing 140
horsepower, teamed with a
three-speed, Synchro-Mesh
manual transmission. Optional
engines ranges up to 283
horsepower.*

3

## Chassis Changes

IN CHASSIS design, Chevrolet held pat. These were
the last Chevys until Corvair to be 115 inches or
less in wheelbase. Fourteen-inch tires lowered the
chassis an inch or so, ball-joint front suspension
was adopted, and new shock absorbers applied.
Revised styling did result in longer cars and an
apparent longer look. A bright array of new upholstery and trim made the 1957 Chevrolet as "new" as
it possibly could be considering the age of its basic
body.

The 1957 Corvette used styling basically the
same as 1956, with an oval grille cavity featuring a
row of vertical teeth, concave side sculpture, sunk-
en taillights, a wrapped windshield and nerf-type
bumpers. The most interest surrounded the Vette

with fuel injection, and magazines hastened to test
examples. *Road & Track* managed to borrow a
four-speed version with FI and Posi-traction (limited slip differential). The editors loved it, and well
they might: it did 0-60 in less than six seconds,
topped 132 miles per hour and covered the standing quarter mile in just 14.3 seconds. "The fuel
injection engine is an absolute jewel," *R & T* ex-
claimed, "quiet and remarkably docile when driven
gently around town, yet instantly transformable
into a roaring brute when pushed hard. Its best
feature is its instantaneous throttle response."

Other magazines were less enthusiastic. *Motor
Trend* called a similar 'Vette "an unhappy, jumpy
little car," and admitted that performance was
fantastic but not all that much better than carburetor versions.

**2**

**4**

**5**

The Automobile Manufacturers Association had passed a resolution in early '57, recommending that manufacturers stay out of direct racing competition. This brought to an end official sponsorship by Chevrolet in the short-track racing it had dominated in 1956. Yet a team of "private" Chevies, using bolt-on performance parts, dominated their class at the NASCAR Speed Weeks, and ran close to 100 mph in the quarter mile at drag strips. One NASCAR two-door with FI turned the quarter in 14 seconds while returning 15 miles per gallon. Chevrolet published a booklet on performance parts, instructing an owner how to make a stormer out of his '57, and many owners did exactly that. Whether they were "official" or not, the 283 V8 Chevrolets became and remained among the more successful cars on drag strip and oval track.

**Nomad's End**

THE LAST of the true Nomad was seen in 1957, although the name was used through 1961. The Nomad was probably the prettiest wagon ever designed, with a beautifully curved roof pillar taken from the L'Universalle show van and two-door hardtop-wagon styling done mainly by Carl Renner. Originally it was to have been a wagon version of the Corvette—a "Corvette Nomad" had appeared at the 1954 Motorama—but cost considerations and slow Corvette sales brought about use of the standard 1954 wagon chassis.

The Nomad was a dramatic car, luxuriously trimmed and beautifully styled from any angle. During 1956 and 1957 it changed gradually to a more "stock" type of car, without the special trim items

The One-Fifty was Chevrolet's economy-priced series in 1957. The Utility Sedan was the lowest-cost model. It was a three-passenger car without a back seat.

that accompanied it in 1955. It always took to the current facelift with ease, remaining beautiful despite annual model updates. It finally succumbed to a combination of high price, low consumer demand and the request by Chevy's force for more practical four-door wagons. Just over 23,000 were built in the three years of Nomad production, with the 1957 model — at 6103 units — the lowest.

For the collector, the Chevrolets are easily the most desirable General Motors cars of 1957. Almost without exception, each model from One-Fifty to Bel Air to Corvette has something to offer, even including the unpretentious One-Fifty sedan delivery. The range of engines, good styling and increasing values make these cars eminently collectible.

## 1957 Chevrolet Division Specifications

| Make and Model | Dimensions | | | | Engines | | | | | | | | Weight lbs. |
| | Wheelbase ins. | Overall Length ins. | Overall Width ins. | Overall Height ins. | 235 cu. in. OHV6 140 Bhp. | 265 cu. in. V8 162 Bhp. | 283 cu. in. V8 185 Bhp. | 283 cu. in. V8 220 Bhp. | 283 cu. in.* V8 245 Bhp. | 283 cu. in. V8 250 Bhp. | 283 cu. in. V8 270 Bhp. | 283 cu. in.* V8 283 Bhp. | |
|---|---|---|---|---|---|---|---|---|---|---|---|---|---|
| Bel Air | 115 | 200 | 73.9 | 59.9 | S | 0 | 0 | 0 | — | — | — | — | 3290 |
| One-Fifty | 115 | 200 | 73.9 | 59.9 | S | 0 | 0 | 0 | — | — | — | — | 3290 |
| Two-Ten | 115 | 200 | 73.9 | 59.9 | S | 0 | 0 | 0 | — | — | — | — | 3300 |
| Six | 115 | 200 | 73.9 | 59.9 | S | 0 | 0 | 0 | — | — | — | — | 2730 |
| Corvette | 102 | 169 | 70 | 51 | — | — | — | S | 0 | 0 | 0 | 0 | 2730 |

*With Ramjet Fuel injection
**Key:** S: Standard Engine  O: Optional Engine     *Variation in horsepower with different engine options.*

# OLDSMOBILE

SOME OF THE most exciting GM show cars were turned out in the Fifties by Oldsmobile, traditionally the "experimental division" of General Motors. It was Oldsmobile that first introduced Hydra-matic transmission back in the late Thirties. In 1948, Oldsmobile displayed the earliest all-postwar GM designs. Olds, along with Cadillac, pioneered the modern overhead valve V8 in 1949. In 1953, low-production harbingers of future GM styling included the Buick Skylark, Cadillac Eldorado and Oldsmobile Fiesta. They featured the first wraparound windshields and beltline dips that would become across-the-board features of GM automobiles by 1955.

During the Fifties, Olds ran off show cars in rapid-fire succession. Along with the Fiesta (which actually saw 458 copies) came the one-off Starfire, a roadster named after a U.S. Air Force fighter; it sported the wide, scoop-type grille/bumper that accurately forecast the 1956 Oldsmobiles. So did the F-88, a Corvette-like sports car, in 1954. Then in 1955 came Delta — low, curvaceous, wide-grilled and with lots of glass. The Delta helped establish the lines of 1957 production Oldsmobiles.

Like Buicks and Cadillacs, Oldsmobiles were all-new in design for 1957 and were advertised as "the most completely redesigned Oldsmobiles in 20 years." The cars shared the General Motors "B" body with the Buick Special and Century, but their mechanical components were all-Oldsmobile.

The line of 88 "Golden Rockets" (a misnomer, because Olds was celebrating its 60th, and not its golden anniversary then) comprised a major increase in available body styles over 1956. Oldsmobile was expanding in an attempt to hold its number five position in the toughening production battle. The division had been in fourth place three years earlier, when Plymouth and Chrysler had teetered near the brink; it had run just short of Plymouth in 1955 and was only 20,000 units away in 1956. On balance, the Olds effort in 1957 was a success: it held on to fifth place and built almost 400,000 vehicles, only 17,000 short of Buick.

## Many Body Types

THE BASIC lineup was scattered over the usual 88, Super 88 and 98 lines, but within those categories there were a wide range of bodies. In 1956, the 88 and Super 88 had offered nine body types between them; in 1957 no less than 13 were offered, with Fiesta station wagons adding liberally to both lines. Prices took a jump too: the cheapest Olds you could buy in 1957 was the 88 two-door at $2733 — over $300 more than it had cost in 1956.

The 1957 Oldsmobiles and other GM "B" bodies

*The most expensive Oldsmobile convertible available in 1957 was the 98 Starfire.*

The 8.5 inches added length on the 98 Starfire put extra room in the car's trunk.

were a bit cleaner than 1956 models, and cleaner by far than their 1958 successors. The wide-scoop grille/bumper that was inspired by the Starfire was still there, deep and recessed, with enclosed circular parking lights. Side-notched headlight hoods and dividers in the rear windows were obvious new features. The longstanding globe with rings was still on the hood, and little rockets rode the front fenders. Beyond this glitter, the Oldsmobile was very clean. There was new side trim, a fully rede-

1

For 1957, the Starfire 98s were the top-of-the-line Oldsmobiles. The 98 Holiday Sedan (1) and the 98 Holiday Coupe (3) came standard with Hydramatic automatic transmission. It was an extra-cost option on Super 88s, including the convertible model (2).

3

signed rear deck, new fenders and bumpers. Two-tone areas were confined to the roof and upper quarters of the rear fenders and deck; this was almost a reversion to the 1953-54 style of two-toning.

The cleanest '57 Olds was the base 88, which showed no series nameplate or bright rocker panel moldings. On other models the curved accent moldings started at the windshield pillars and slanted rearward and downward; on the 88 they began near the center of the door on two-door models and the front edge of the rear door on four-door models. The 88 also benefited from the engine used in the larger cars, making it a "best buy" for 1957.

The Super 88 was identified by nameplates on its front fenders, but had painted rocker panels like the 88. The side windows were chrome trimmed on hardtops, paint trimmed on sedans. The 98, in contrast, used bright metal rocker panel moldings and all models, including the sedans, had bright trim around windows.

Oldsmobile interiors benefited from themes laid down by the Delta show car. The instrument panel exhibited several unique innovations, although whether or not they were improvements is debatable. The instruments were grouped in an oval pod

under the wheel, and utilized a printed circuit (an Oldsmobile first) instead of the usual jungle of wires found behind typical dashboards. Like in the Delta, the top of the dash featured a large gap between the panel and the windshield frame. A plus was Olds' new dual heater. One unit was mounted under each side of the dash, allowing driver and passenger to set their own temperature preference.

**Good Performers**

OLDSMOBILES for 1957 were good-performing cars—not up to the Buick Century standard, but more than a match for most of their rivals. The Super 88 hardtop, for example, did the 0-60 run in less than ten seconds and hit 77 mph in 17.7 seconds for the standing quarter mile, while giving fuel mileage of 14 miles per gallon in a day of 20-cent per gallon gasoline. Most testers felt it would do 115 miles an hour. However, the Super 88's traditional performance "plus" had been eliminated by Oldsmobile's decision to use one engine for all three models. For the past few years the Super, like Buick's Century, had enjoyed a senior engine in a junior body. It had been the hot rod of the group. In 1957 the 277 hp V8 was applied throughout the Olds line, giving the plain 88 as much power as the

2

The name "Super 88" might suggest more engine power, but all Oldsmobiles had the same 277-horsepower engine. The Super 88 was actually a middle model in the Olds lineup for 1957. Olds offered a full range of body styles in the Super 88 line, including the four-door sedan (1), the two-door hardtop (2) and the wagon (3). Jetaway Hydra-matic transmission, which was standard in the 98 models, was an 88 option.

Super. The engine was considerably enlarged over 1956, and had higher compression than ever before in Oldsmobile history.

Road testers agreed that Oldsmobile handling ranked high in 1957, crediting this to its new "Wide-Stance" chassis and heavier frame construction. Oldsmobile had switched to ball-joint front suspension in '57, although the frame was still the cow-belly type rather than the new X-shape of Cadillac. Some writers pointed out that the roadability qualities were not as noticeable on the '57 Oldsmobile because the make had been high in this respect for the past several years. In the early Fifties, Rocket 88s had dominated NASCAR and AAA ovals, burning up the turf and setting new records at every outing. The auto manufacturers had told the

1

2

3

world they were through with racing in 1957, but the 88 was remembered nevertheless — and it was still a fast car.

A growing Oldsmobile owners club will no doubt make the 1957 models popular as collectors items in time, but no great movement surrounds them at present. As is normally the case with all old cars, convertibles are the rarest and the most desirable,

followed by hardtops. The wagons are a bit bulky, but interesting because they were the first Olds wagons in seven years — precursors of the new, deluxe, hardtop-styled wagons of the late Fifties. (As were Buick's Caballeros, the wagons were offered in pillar sedan form, though unlike the Buicks they rode on 14-inch tires.)

In the show car department, Oldsmobile was

## 1957 Oldsmobile Division Specifications

| Make and Model | Dimensions | | | | Engines | | | Weight lbs. |
| --- | --- | --- | --- | --- | --- | --- | --- | --- |
| | Wheelbase ins. | Overall Length ins. | Overall Width ins. | Overall Height ins. | 271 cu. in. V8 277 Bhp. | 371 cu. in. V8 J-2 300 Bhp. | 371 cu. in. V8 J-2 312 Bhp. | |
| 88 | 122 | 208.2 | 76.4 | 58.2 | S | O | O | 4000 |
| Super 88 | 122 | 208.2 | 76.4 | 58.2 | S | O | O | 4049 |
| Starfire 98 | 126 | 216.7 | 76.4 | 58.2 | S | O | O | 4347 |

**Key:** *S: Standard Engine  O: Optional Engine*

uncharacteristically passive in 1957, but this was common to all of GM that year. Before the year was out, Olds was breaking new ground again with its Fiesta Carousel wagon and two Harley Earl sports cars, the F-88 Marks II and III. The latter used a retractable hardtop and was taken by Earl when he retired at the end of 1958. The '58 production Oldsmobiles were marked by some of the most garish styling ever put on automobiles. (Ford's Alex Tremulis drew an 88 tail with its four horizontal chrome strips and satirically decorated them with a treble clef and musical notes.) The year 1957 remains one of praiseworthy styling for the Lansing, Michigan division. The '57 Oldsmobiles have potential as future collector cars—more than any other 1957 GM cars except Chevrolet.

*Even Oldsmobile's low-line Golden Rocket 88, including the Holiday Sedan (above), was available with the division's largest engine in 1957.*

# PONTIAC

**P**ONTIAC'S performance-car image was born in 1957. Semon E. "Bunky" Knudsen had taken over as general manager the year before; and although the division was required to live with a facelift for '57, Knudsen decreed that the staid old image of Pontiac had to go. Thus vanished the old silver streaks that had decorated Pontiacs since Virgil Exner invented them around 1935. Although the basic "A" body shells (even with new 14-inch tires) were as much as five inches higher than restyled competition from Mercury and Dodge, the new Pontiacs looked about as different as they could by virtue of clever styling tricks that emphasized length and lowness.

The Pontiacs of 1955-56 were good-handling cars, but they had a notoriously hard ride. Despite Knudsen's performance push, something had to be done about those bumps. The '57s consequently ran very long, with 60-inch rear springs mounted in rubber shackles. Front end specifications were not altered, and Pontiac refused to join its GM cousins in the shift to ball-joint front suspension.

The old body dictated that wheelbases remain at the same 122 inches for Chieftain and Super Chief and 124 inches for Star Chief as in 1956, but the new 14-inch tires lowered the body a bit. Features of higher-priced Buicks were found in the foot pedal parking brake and an automatic electric radio antenna that extended when the set was turned on and retracted when it was turned off.

Pontiac styling was fairly clean for the period and better than in the previous two years, except for a front end that bore a massive bumper/grille and a resemblance to an electric shaver. The previous year's marque emblem of inverted "V" and circle was retained, and Chief Pontiac's head appeared on each fender. Instead of two-tone panels on the upper body from the cowl back as per 1955-56, the '57 Pontiac used a simple sweep spear painted the same color as the roof.

**Price Ranges**

PONTIAC'S Series 27 followed a GM trend with

*Updated '56-style side trim appears on the early '57 Pontiac prototype. Pontiac was not due to receive drastic style changes until 1958, but the facelift was successful.*

The classy Pontiac Bonneville (1) was introduced later in '57 to join the Star Chief, Pontiac's top model. The wheelbase of the Star Chief was two inches longer than that of other models, and it was seven inches longer overall than the Chieftain and Super Chief. Star Chiefs included the two-door (2) and four-door (3) models. Both were hardtops.

▲ Star Chiefs such as the convertible had luxurious interiors featuring leather or leather/nylon combination.

The rear end of the Star Chief was not exactly trim, but it was impressive. Exhaust pipes were integral ▼ with the bumper.

prices ranging from $200-$300 higher than those of the previous year. The Chieftan and Super Chief differed mainly in trim and price. There were 12 different models altogether, including four kinds of Catalina hardtop and five different Safari station wagons. The usual brace of two- and four-door sedans also were offered. The only Pontiac convertible was in the senior, 124-inch wheelbase Series 28.

Both Chieftain and Super Chief used three stars in the side spear and bore series nameplates on their front fenders. Super Chief was distinguished by "wavy grid" Morrokide upholstery in hardtops and sedans, and factory-fitted rear fender skirts.

Series 28 Star Chiefs came in five models, including two hardtops and a convertible, but no station wagon. They wore an extra star in their side

spears, testifying, no doubt, to superior rank. The Custom four-door sedan used "off shoulder" interior styling: wide leather panels at the top of backrests were asymmetrically placed on one side of the car. Morrokide backrests similar to the lower priced Super Chief's were found on the Deluxe four-door sedan.

A brand-new Pontiac stressing Knudsen's interest in performance was the Bonneville, a potent convertible stormer on the 124-inch wheelbase. It was a supercar with 310 horsepower, hydraulic lifters, high-lift cam, and fuel injection. This big, semi-custom (only 630 built) ragtop sold for close to $6000 and delivered the best performance that fuel injection could provide. It was named for the salt flats in Utah where land speed records had been

The 1957 Star Chief line included four-door models in a hardtop style (shown here) and a pillared sedan style. A two-door pillared sedan was not offered, although a two-door hardtop was.

set. Knudsen said it might set some records in its own class, given the opportunity.

A Bonneville was tested by an automotive magazine over a 138-mile simulated economy run. It averaged 41 miles per hour and scored 17.2 miles per gallon. This was somewhat below standard Pontiac economy, but not bad for a 310 hp car capable of tremendous acceleration and a high top speed. The best the Bonneville would do in the standing quarter mile was 18 seconds, according to the magazine's editors, while the optional Tri-Power setup (three two-barrel carburetors) had been reported to turn the quarter in 16.8 seconds. The editors concluded that Pontiac had purposely held onto Tri-Power in anticipation of production and service problems with fuel injection. There

Unlike cars that underwent complete styling changes in 1957, the four-door Pontiac Chieftain sedan appeared tall and stodgy. Chieftain was the lowest-priced '57 Pontiac.

1

2

Looking at the 1957 Pontiac models like the four-door Star Chief sedan (1) and four-door hardtop (2) gives little feeling of race-car power. But Pontiac proved itself in the 1957 Daytona 150 (3), when three '57 Pontiacs and a lonely Chevy led the pack. Cotton Owens, in the lead car, won the race. Banjo Matthews in Car No. 8 and Darel Dieringer in No. 85 snapped at the tail of the Chevy, driven by Jack Smith.

3

were problems—dirty jets, reluctance to accept certain fuels, confusing performance effects depending on injector nozzles used. In the long run, fuel injection was dropped until recent years when federal emissions standards made it the only way to go on some cars, in order to comply with the law or achieve driveability.

### Engine Packages

THE STANDARD line of Pontiacs all ran the same 347 cubic-inch V8 as the Bonneville—detuned, of course. The engine had jumped 30 cubic-inches from 1956 and had new manifolds and combustion chambers, larger valves and higher compression. Three basic power packages were offered: 227 hp for manual shift cars, 252 for Chieftains with automatic, and 270 for Super Chiefs and Star Chiefs. Dual exhausts were optional. A small innovation was the vented valve guide, a narrow hole drilled in the head, connected to an intake valve stem and vented to the atmosphere. The suction built up by manifold pressure on deceleration was thereby eliminated. Pontiac's Hydra-matic transmission

*Both Star Chiefs and Super Chiefs, like the four-door sedan (1), were equipped with a 347 cubic-inch V8 (2) that put out 270 horsepower. The engine had a unique feature: its intake valve stems were vented to atmospheric pressure. Safari wagons were available in all three series. They shared taillight design with other models (3).*

was beefed up to cope with the larger, more powerful 1957 engines, and a transmission oil cooler was now integral with the main radiator.

Engineering progress notwithstanding, Pontiac was still stuck with the same body. However, this did not hurt sales. In a year that saw Chevy production drop by 100,000, Buick by 125,000, and Oldsmobile by 42,000, Pontiac built 343,298 cars and moved close to Oldsmobile by increasing its output 10,000 units over 1956. Except for Cadillac, this was the only GM division to build more cars in 1957 than in 1956—the only medium-priced car not to

suffer from strong efforts by Ford, Chrysler and AMC. For Pontiac, therefore, 1957 was a satisfactory year. It was also the beginning of the Knudsen revolution, which had its climax in 1962 when Pontiac built a record 550,000 cars and climbed unopposed into third place.

Collectible Pontiacs from 1957 are scarce. The only two of historic merit are the Bonneville, and Pontiac's version of the Chevy Nomad two-door wagon, called the Safari. The Bonneville is important as the first true performance Pontiac, the Safari because it's pretty but rare.

## 1957 Pontiac Division Specifications

| Make and Model | Dimensions | | | | Engines* | | | Weight lbs. |
| | Wheelbase ins. | Overall Length ins. | Overall Width ins. | Overall Height ins. | 347 cu. in. V8 227 Bhp. | 347 cu. in. V8 252 Bhp. | 347 cu. in. V8 270 Bhp. | |
| --- | --- | --- | --- | --- | --- | --- | --- | --- |
| Chieftan | 122 | 206.8 | 72.5 | 60.7 | S | 0 | — | 3685 |
| Super Chief | 122 | 206.8 | 72.5 | 60.7 | — | — | S | 3635 |
| Star Chief | 124 | 213.8 | 72.5 | 60.1 | — | — | S | 3635 |
| Bonneville | 124 | 213.8 | 72.5 | 60.7 | — | — | S | 4285 |

**Key:** S: Standard Engine  O: Optional Engine          *Variation in horsepower with different engine options.

*In 1957, all Pontiac station wagons carried the name Safari, even the four-door models like this Super Chief.*

The retractable-hardtop Fairlane 500 Skyliner was a failure. The retracting system lacked dependibility.

AS FAR BACK as 1957, Henry Ford II was believed to have inherited more than just his name from his grandfather; he was noted for good business sense and marketing savvy. So when the president of Ford Motor Company introduced the '57 models, people listened.

Ford said, "... To bring out a completely new car this year—only two years after the complete 1955 change—has cost the company a lot of money, more than any other introduction in our history." He went on, "The 1957 Ford has been ten years in the making. It is the crowning achievement of our post-war resurgence ... This is the year we've been aiming for."

The public would prove Ford's aim to be right on target. The 1957 line of Ford-built cars—the Fords that Henry Ford II introduced, the new-from-the-ground-up Mercurys and the Lincolns—struck the American public's fancy. The cars were longer and lower; the look was enhanced by rear-fender fins and hooded headlamps on some models. The new styling was symbolic of a new corporate style. Henry Ford II and his management team had begun a

new era of leadership, and it paid off. That model year, for the first time since 1935, Ford outsold Chevrolet.

Ford and his board chairman Ernest R. Breech were calling the corporate shots with help from a number of industry stalwarts. They included Lewis D. Crusoe, James J. Nance, George W. Walker, and "Whiz Kids" Arjay R. Miller (later company president), Francis C. Reith, Ben D. Mills, James O. Wright and the fast-rising Robert S. McNamara.

**Crusoe's Assignment**

WHEN CRUSOE was named head of the newly formed Ford Division in 1949, Ford and Breech had given him one assignment: beat Chevrolet. By 1953, during the 1957-model planning stages, Crusoe and his division were ready to make their bid. Crusoe took a look at the market, which was headed by Chevrolet and Ford, and saw the larger Buick in third place. It had replaced the third member of the "low-priced three," Plymouth. By 1954, Buick's 500,000-unit sales volume had allowed that

# FORD MOTOR COMPANY

sidered to be at the low end of the upper-priced field. In the $2400 to $3100 price range, GM was marketing three cars, Chrysler two and Ford none. When Crusoe was named executive vice president of Ford's Car and Truck Division in 1955, he had appointed Francis C. Reith to his staff. Reith was noted for his Ford achievements in France. In making the appointment, Crusoe said Reith had been chosen to help formulate Ford's "important forward planning." That planning began almost immediately.

In April of 1955, Reith presented to the Ford board of directors an all-encompassing plan to improve the company's future products. He proposed a better balance of small cars, medium and higher-priced cars, with the new E-Car providing that balance. He suggested that the E-Car be built on two different shells—a lower-priced version on the Ford shell and a higher-priced model on the Mercury shell. The proposal got Crusoe's nod and the board of directors approved the plan.

**Plans for Split**

MEANWHILE, in those planning days for the 1957 models, a bold corporate decision was being made to split Ford Motor Company into four divisions like GM. Ford Division would expand its 1957 product line to two wheelbases, Custom and Fairlane; Mercury and Lincoln would split; and, because the E-Car was already nearing reality, a separate division would be formed and named Edsel after that new car. The company later returned to two divisions, but the results of the split proved beneficial to long-term corporate planning.

Ford's move upward in the market had a staggering effect on the industry. As Ford was building its bigger car, Chrysler was making similar plans of its own, reasoning that the only way to lower each car's cost was to design all of the corporation's models with greater parts interchangeability. By interchanging Plymouth parts (primarily bodies and doors) with Dodge and Chrysler, top manage-

GM division to build a bigger car at a relatively low price. Crusoe's conclusion was that the public wanted bigger cars. Times were good and people were willing to pay a little more to get a nicer package. Crusoe noted that Mercury, after 15 years on the market, had not met the Buick-Oldsmobile-Pontiac challenge. There was only one answer: beef up the Ford.

Even before the 1950s it was clear that Americans were looking for more luxury in their cars. By the middle of the decade, power accessories—steering, windows, brakes, and seats—were being offered even in the lower-priced models. Ford division officials had scoffed at smaller cars of the early '50s, such as the Henry J, Rambler, and the Hudson Jet. Ford management had boasted, "To the average American our present car and its size represent an outward symbol of prestige and well being." Crusoe had called the lower-priced Ford "practically non-saleable. People do not want it."

Sales dropped in the lower-priced segment as the public sought more motoring luxury. So, along with beefing up the Ford, top company management was in the mood for an all-new car to compete in the medium-priced area. Mercury was con-

*Production Skyliners differed slightly from an early mockup (above), but poor public relations brought about the model's demise. Ford had hoped to corner the retractable-hardtop market.*

ment would be upsizing the low-priced Plymouth and asking a higher price. Some Chrysler executives initially balked at this line of thinking, but decided to make the move when word leaked out that Ford also was upsizing its low-priced models.

When two of the low-priced three boosted prices for their cars, consumers reacted by buying them. When sales figures were totaled at the end of the '57 model year, Crusoe's mission was accomplished; Ford had beaten Chevrolet 1.49 million units to 1.45 million. It was to happen only once again, in 1959. The trend toward bigger cars would continue for 20 years.

Ford Division General Manager Robert McNamara told the press in September 1956 that his division's forecasts called for at least a ten percent increase in production and an even greater increase in Ford car sales. This increase, McNamara said, would continue the trend of 1956 when the Ford car gained a higher percentage of the market than it had in 1955, despite the fact that total industry sales in 1956 declined from the record 1955 levels. Sales did climb back up in 1957 and, true to McNamara's word, Ford gained a higher percentage of the market—24.97 to Chevy's 24.34. Most importantly, however, Ford had succeeded in letting the world know that its new management team was able to meet the challenge of the marketplace.

**Ranchero Debuts**

BESIDES THE longer, lower bodies and streamlined design by styling director George Walker and his staff, Ford introduced a new concept in combination vehicles—the Ford Ranchero. This passenger car/pickup truck set a pattern in the industry by offering the styling of a car and the versatility of a pickup. A publicity release described the vehicle this way: "The Ranchero, sixteen inches lower and eighteen inches longer than a 1956 Ford pickup, resembles the new Ford passenger car from the front bumper to the vehicle's midpoint. But from the midpoint to the rear, the vehicle is a highly styled pickup truck with greater load space and a lower loading height." Chevrolet later followed with a similar type vehicle, but Ford had added another achievement—a new vehicle that found its own place in the hearts and minds of the public.

The Thunderbird, Ford's earlier masterpiece, had followed Chevy's Corvette to the marketplace and quickly outdistanced the GM sports model. Late in 1957, the two-passenger success became a four-seater, and the T-Bird rolled on and on to bigger dimensions and greater demand.

But in the midst of these successes, other Ford-built products were having their problems. Mercury and the short-lived Ford retractable hardtop were losers. The Mercury, with sloping rear-fender fins and hooded headlamps, suffered serious sales setbacks, especially in its innovative Turnpike Cruiser model. At the same time, Ford Division's attempt to corner a new market on hardtop convertibles died a quick death. From its inception, the "metal car that swallows its top" had a terminal illness: poor quality.

And a true disaster was ready to debut. In September 1957, shortly before the rest of the 1958 model line was shown to the public, the E Car Edsel was introduced. The recession of 1958 doomed the medium-priced car even before it ran into such problems as a confused public (confused as to what price range the car fit into), a crowded market segment, too many defects and a public snubbing of the horse-collar grille. Production of the Edsel was discontinued before the end of 1959.

# FORD

FROM EARLY in its planning stages, the '57 Ford was scheduled to be longer and lower, as most other models that year, yet bigger, with a bigger price. Because the American car-buying public was looking for more luxury in automobiles, and because the larger, higher-priced Buick was taking sales from the so-called low-priced three, Ford Division chief Robert S. McNamara and other top Ford executives took the '57 Ford to two different sizes—a first for Ford.

After using a 115-inch wheelbase on all 1956 models, Ford offered the Custom and Custom 300 series with a 116-inch wheelbase and the Fairlane and Fairlane 500 series with a 118-inch wheelbase. Overall length of the Custom series was three inches more than the '56 model; the Fairlane was nine inches longer. Height was lowered three to four inches. More important than a comparison with its predecessor was how it stacked up to its competition, Chevrolet. Ford was two inches long-er, three inches wider and three inches lower than the car that had held the number one sales position for so long. Ford's standard V8 boasted a 190-horsepower rating to Chevy's 162 hp. Ford's 1957 model sales hit 1.49 million to Chevy's 1.45 million.

The 21 Ford models, including the Thunderbird, featured 14-inch wheels. This helped to lower the overall height. Also, a depressed floor pan compensated for headroom that would have been cut by the lower roof. Overall height for the '57 Custom was 57.2 inches; Fairlane was 56.2 inches. Front headroom was advertised as 33.5 inches in the Custom and 34.5 in the Fairlane (compared with 34.9 in the '56 Customline). Sales brochures showed rear headroom at 33.5 inches in the Custom and 34.5 in the Fairlane (compared with 33.9 the previous year). Overall length increased from 198.5 on the '56 Customline to 201.7 on the '57 Custom and 207.7 on the '57 Fairlane.

*The 1957 Thunderbird's bumper-to-bumper length shrank. Its body length increased, however, because of the elimination of the outside-mounted spare incorporated in 1956 models.*

Ford offered both rag-top convertible and retractable-hardtop models in 1957. Customer preference leaned away from the more expensive hardtop Skyliner (1 and 2), but the rag-top Sunliner (3) was popular.

*The profile of the Fairlane 500 Town Victoria four-door hardtop exemplified the 1957 Ford's long, low look. It was two inches longer and three inches lower than a 1957 Chevrolet.*

## Model Offerings

FORD OFFERED three sedan models in the Custom series; two Custom 300 sedans; four Fairlanes (two sedans and two hardtops); and five models in the Fairlane 500 series, two sedans, two hardtops and the Sunliner convertible. Three engines were available in each series. The Customs offered the Thunderbird 312 Special 245 hp, the standard Ford 272 V8, 190 hp; and the new Mileage Maker Six, 144 hp. The Fairlanes substituted the Thunderbird 212 hp

292 V8 for the 272-CID engine as standard equipment; the other two optional engines were the same as in the Customs.

New features included high-canted rear fins, thin-pillar sedans ("hardtop styling at lower cost," boasted the ads), swept-back windshield pillars, tapered vent windows, and visor-type roof extensions on front and rear.

With all the new styling and engineering features on the '57 Fords, the biggest news was the special model that Ford advertised as " one of the most

*Fairlane and Fairlane 500 models, such as the Club Victoria two-door hardtop, shared a 118-inch wheelbase. The wheelbase of Custom and Custom 500 models was shorter--116 inches.*

One of Ford's successful innovations in 1957 was thin-window-pillar design, illustrated by the Fairlane 500 Club Sedan (1) and Fairlane Town Sedan (3). Ford's aim was to offer styling similar to its hardtop models, including the Fairlane Club Victoria (2), at a more economical price.

remarkable automobile bodies ever offered to the public — the new Ford retractable hardtop." One description of the Fairlane 500 Skyliner's top-down cycle explained: "Stowing the top is as easy as taking off your hat. A dashboard button, working only when the car is in neutral, activates the first of seven electric motors, raising the deck lid. Next the top is automatically released and finally comes to rest inside the luggage compartment. When the top has been completely swallowed, the deck lid comes down. The entire cycle takes fifty seconds or less." The problem, of course, was that it rarely worked. There were too many bugs in the retractable hardtop model and the car lasted less than three years. However, the hardtop-convertible was about the only Ford that did not sell that year.

**Strength of Wagons**

WHEN FORD took over sales leadership from

Custom 300 models like the Fordor Sedan (1) and the Tudor Sedan (3) were the same size as Custom models, but had more extensive exterior trim and interior appointments. The Custom found favor with the stock-car set. A 312 cubic-inch supercharged-V8 powered the Custom driven by Marvin Panch at Daytona in 1957 (2).

Chevrolet, it did so with the help of 320,000 station wagons. The Ford wagon's styling was a high point: it was recognized as one of the best-designed wagons on the market. The popular six-passenger Country Sedan, which more than 130,000 customers bought, ranked fifth in sales among the entire 21-model Ford line. Four other station wagons were offered in 1957: the two-door, economy-priced Ranch Wagon, about $2400, the two-door intermediate Del Rio Ranch Wagon, a dressed-up standard Ranch Wagon at about $2500; the four-door nine-passenger Country Sedan, about $2650; and the four-door, nine-passenger Country Squire with wood panelling, almost $2800.

The six-passenger Country Sedan was 3-1/2 inches lower than its '56 counterpart, while overall length was increased about six inches. Wheelbase was increased to the Custom-sized 116 inches. The engines available in the Fairlane and Fairlane 500 series were offered in the wagons; the optional

Thunderbird 312 Special V8, 245 hp; Thunderbird 292 V8, 212 hp; and the standard Mileage Maker Six, 144 hp.

The 1957 wagons featured a completely new lift-gate and tailgate structure with a single, lift-type latch release. More cargo space was added to the '57 versions of the six-passenger wagons by allowing the rear cushion and rear seat to fold flat, forming part of the load space.

Another new vehicle in 1957 did not quite fit into the car line, and certainly did not count in the total car sales figures, but it was another industry first for Ford and played a role similar to that of the station wagon. The Ranchero, a half-ton pickup, made its debut in November, 1956, with this announcement: "A completely new kind of commercial vehicle—one that looks, rides and handles like a passenger car but does the work of a pickup truck—was unveiled today for the first time in automotive history . . ." The Ranchero was 16 inches

*Wagon sales hit 320,000 for Ford in 1957. The most luxurious wagon was the nine-passenger Country Squire with wood paneling (1 and 2). The rear of the car featured the new single-latch tailgate. The price of the nine-passenger Country Sedan (3) was about $150 lower than the fancier Country Squire which retailed for $2800.*

lower and 18 inches longer than the 1956 Ford pickup. With interiors the same as in the station wagon, the Ranchero looked like a passenger car with a pickup bed. It was offered with standard, overdrive or Fordomatic transmissions. Two models were available: Ranchero, with the 272 V8, 190 hp; and Custom Ranchero, with the Thunderbird 292 V8, 212 hp. Each also was available with the new 144 hp Mileage Maker Six.

Both the Ford station wagons and the Ranchero offered car buyers a wide range of choices in utility vehicles. They were stylized versions of transportation that could get the job done, and they found their niche in the marketplace.

### Thunderbird's Ride

ANOTHER NICHE was occupied by Thunderbird. Car buffs gave almost immediate recognition to the 1957 T-Bird, the last of the three-year line of classic

*The Ford Ranchero (1) made its debut in 1957. The half-ton utility vehicle was 16 inches lower and 18 inches longer than a '56 Ford pickup. Two-door wagons like the Del Rio Ranch Wagon (2) featured a back seat that folded down flat with the floor. The portholed roof was one feature carried over from 1956 in the hardtop Thunderbird (3).*

*The 1957 Ford Thunderbird featured new tailfins and an extended rear deck.*

did most other '57 models. The rear deck was longer and the outside spare that distinguished the '56 version was gone. Thunderbird for '57 continued with two models, the convertible coupe and hardtop. The hardtop maintained the side porthole it had developed the previous year. Wheelbase remained at 102 inches, but overall bumper-to-bumper length was reduced by about four inches and the body was lengthened by 5-1/2 inches when the T-Bird's outside spare tire was moved to the trunk.

The 1957 Thunderbird offered a choice of three engines: the Thunderbird 292 V8 two-barrel, 212 hp; T-Bird 312 Special V8 four-barrel 245 hp; and T-Bird 312 Super V8 four-barrel, 265 hp.

A wider checkerboard grille and standard padded sun visors were new features boasted by Thunderbird. Optional features included a new power seat with seven horizontal and five vertical positions (with control on the instrument panel). This option contained a "memory" system that brought the seat to the driver's selected position whenever the ignition was turned on. When the ignition was turned off, the seat was designed to return to its rear-most position. Another option to attract luxury seekers was an automatic volume control on the radio. Sales brochures promised, "The volume of sound will start increasing from ten miles per hour and continue up to sixty mph in order to compensate for increases in wind and road noise." The industry's struggle to come up with newer luxury equipment, as well as bigger and better cars, continued for the remainder of the Fifties. The Thunderbirds—new and old—continued as a car in demand.

two-seaters. When the 1958 four-passenger model was announced, the 21,000 two-seaters were already in great demand—a demand that has grown considerably with the years. The 1957 T-Bird retailed for about $3400. By 1963, its average used car price was $1740 (while the six-year-old Ford was going for $550), although buffs were paying $3000 for those T-Birds in good shape. Today, you still can get a decent '57 two-seater for about $4000, pay up to $8000 if it has been restored, and spend as much as $30,000 for a top show car. The super sports model had been introduced in 1954 to counter Chevy's Corvette. It succeeded beyond its backers' wildest expectations, soaring to more than 50,000 sales in its first three years.

When the '57 model was introduced in the fall of 1956, it boasted rear-fender fins and a lower look as

## 1957 Ford Specifications

| Make and Model | Dimensions | | | | Engines* | | | | | | | Weight lbs. |
|---|---|---|---|---|---|---|---|---|---|---|---|---|
| | Wheelbase ins. | Overall Length ins. | Overall Width ins. | Overall Height ins. | 223 cu. in. Six 144 Bhp. | 292 cu. in. V8 205 Bhp. | 272 cu. in. V8 190 Bhp. | 312 cu. in. V8 212 Bhp. | 312 cu. in. V8 245 Bhp. | 312 cu. in. V8 265 Bhp. | 312 cu. in. V8 300 Bhp. | |
| Custom | 116 | 201.7 | 77 | 57.2 | O | — | S | — | O | O | O | 3472 |
| Custom 300 | 116 | 201.7 | 77 | 57.2 | — | — | S | — | O | O | O | 3472 |
| Fairlane | 118 | 207.9 | 77 | 56.2 | — | O | — | S | O | O | O | 3472 |
| Fairlane 500 | 118 | 207.9 | 77 | 56.2 | — | — | — | S | O | O | O | 3472 |
| Fairlane 500 Skyliner | 118 | 77 | 77 | 56.2 | — | — | — | S | O | O | O | 3472 |
| Thunderbird | 102 | 181 | 73 | 56.2 | — | S | — | — | O | O | O | 3145 |
| Thunderbird Special | 102 | 181 | 73 | 56.2 | — | S | — | — | O | O | O | 3145 |
| Six | 116 | 202 | 77 | 57 | S | — | — | — | — | — | — | 3472 |

**Key:** *S: Standard Engine   O: Optional Engine   *Variation in horsepower with different engine options.*

# LINCOLN

DESPITE THE FACT that the 1957 Lincoln was a pleasing car, it suffered a sales setback; production fell from more than 50,000 in 1956 to about 40,000, a 20 percent decrease. Lincoln Division had been a separate organization for only two years, and it was to be reunited with Mercury Division during '57. As Henry Ford II has said, "Things just didn't work out." There were many reasons for the move back to one division, not the least of which was the need to restructure, then eliminate, Edsel responsibilities. Also, Mercury was to be placed back on one shell, instead of the two bodies it used during the 1957 model year. In short, some of the company's bold experiments paid off and some did not; but management responded quickly and kept the company in a solid competitive position.

The most notable differences between the 1956 and 1957 Lincolns were changes in the rear fender and front end. Wide, flaring rear fenders featured canted taillights, and the backup lights were slotted into bumper ovals. The new front end featured quad headlights for the first time, extra-wide parking and signal lights, and a combination bumper grille. A simulated air scoop just in front of the rear wheels also was new. The car was built on the same 126-inch wheelbase as the previous year, but it was almost two inches longer than the '56 model because of the redesigned bumpers. Like most cars of its day, Lincoln highlighted its fins and longer, lower look. One ad talked about the "the poised-for-action flare of the rear blades," and emphasized that "this is the longest, lowest, most powerful Lincoln ever built." The power was there. The 368 cubic-inch engine developed up to 300 horsepower, compared with 285 hp the previous year.

Because of the major change made in the 1956 model, Lincoln only modified its base body in '57. Two series were offered, the Capri and the Premiere. Models in the Capri series were a four-door sedan, four-door Landau hardtop and two-door hardtop. Four models in the Premiere series included the same three as in the Capri series, plus the heaviest (4676 pounds), most expensive (about $5400) Lincoln—the Premiere convertible. The

*Lincoln offered two series in 1957. One of them was the Capri series, including the four-door sedan (above). The other was the Premiere, which outsold the Capri.*

*Although built in 1957, The Mark II (left) shows none of the finned, flashy style of other '57 luxury cars such as the Lincoln Premiere four-door hardtop (right). Poor sales resulted.*

four-door hardtop was new to the Lincoln line. Although the Premiere four-door sedan carried a $500 higher price tag, its chrome rocker panels and Premiere signature on the front fender were all that distinguished it from the lower-priced Capri. The Premiere signature however, had a significant effect on enough buyers to give Premiere nearly 10,000 more sales than Capri in the Landau line, nearly 4000 more four-door sedans, and about 12,000 more two-door hardtops.

**Mark II**

WHEN THE FIRST Mark II was introduced to the public in October 1955, as a limited-edition,

## 1957 Lincoln Specifications

| Make and Model | Dimensions | | | | Engines | Weight lbs. |
|---|---|---|---|---|---|---|
| | Wheelbase Ins. | Overall Length Ins. | Overall Width Ins. | Overall Height Ins. | 368 cu. In. V8 300 Bhp | |
| Capri | 126 | 224.6 | 80.3 | 60.2 | S | 4620 |
| Premiere | 126 | 224.6 | 80.3 | 60.2 | S | 4620 |

**Key:** *S: Standard Engine*

$10,000 luxury coupe, it marked the return of the Continental after a seven-year absence. Never intended to attain a high volume of sales, the Mark II was produced in limited quantity as a prestige automobile. William Clay Ford, general manager of the Continental Division, explained at the time: "The Continental is designed for an exclusive market—a prestige market—consisting of persons with good taste who want an automobile embodying distinction, luxury, dignity and quality."

The original Lincoln Continental had been conceived by and built for William Clay Ford's father, Edsel, in early 1939. After a trip to Florida, Edsel Ford returned with more than 200 orders for the car. In October 1939, the first production Lincoln Continental (a 1940 model) was introduced. A Ford brochure at the time explained that "Body components of regular production model Lincolns were cobbled by hand craftsmen to rigid specifications." Quality and simplicity became synonymous with Continental. In 1951, the car was to be honored by the Museum of Modern Art in New York City. In a special exhibition, the car was displayed with the following tribute: "The Continental satisfied the requirements of connoisseurs while capturing the imagination of a public less preoccupied with the refinements of automobile design."

Mark II was designed to carry on that Continental image; the styling was subtle. The clean lines were set off by the four-pointed-star hood ornament. Only a two-door, four-passenger version was produced. It was originally designated just "Mark II," rather than given a particular model year designation. About 3000 were built between June 1955 and May 1957. The car introduced several features

The Continental Mark II carried an original price tag of $10,000. It was phased out in May, 1957. Although its retail price dipped sharply soon after production ceased, a show-condition model today can cost as much as $15,000.

▲ *In 1957, buyers preferred the higher-priced Lincoln Premiere, including the two-door hardtop model, over Lincoln's Capri.*

*Of all the 1957 Lincolns, the Premiere Convertible* ▼ *was the heftiest and carried the biggest price tag.*

which were incorporated in later Lincoln Continentals, including rear fender treatment, rear taillight and bumper styling, and the deep honeycombed grille.

The 1957 model was built on a 126-inch wheelbase; it was 218.4 inches long and 56 inches high. The hood was almost six feet long. The 368 CID engine (same as Lincoln for that year) developed nearly 300 horsepower, slightly more than the models built in 1956. New to the auto industry was Mark II's self-regulating clock, which, according to Ford literature, "automatically corrects itself by adjusting its rate of speed when the hands are set."

Mark II retailed for $10,000, but near the end of its third year—when the company decided to phase it out—some dealers were finding it difficult to sell the car at list price. A few years later, it still was just another used car. Used car guidebooks in mid-1961 listed the model at $3750; six months later at $500 less. Prices increased gradually starting about ten years ago, but, as recently as four years ago, a clean Mark II sold for only $4000. Then, prices really started to increase. Today, a one-owner Mark II with about 40,000 miles on it—in good condition, but not detailed—could sell for $10,000; a top show car for about $15,000. Some Mark II ads in current car buff magazines describe the car as "a good investment."

# MERCURY

THE STYLING of the 1956 Mercury disappeared without a trace when the 1957 edition made its debut. Under Francis C. Reith, the '57 model was a completely new car, without a hint of its previous styling. Public reaction was not good. Sales dipped about 275,000 from the record 400,000 in 1955.

Mercury had its own shell for the first time (which did not last long), built on a 122-inch wheelbase, three inches longer than the '56 version. The '57 line also included new features such as 14-inch wheels, pushbutton-operated automatic transmission controls on the dash, air-cushion rear suspension system, and power tailgate window lifts on the station wagons.

The new body carried 18 models in four series: the economy Monterey, intermediate Montclair, the infamous Turnpike Cruiser luxury model, and station wagons. In the Monterey series, five models were offered: Phaeton sedan, a four-door hardtop;

Phaeton coupe, a two-door hardtop; convertible; four-door sedan; and two-door sedan. The four-model Montclair series included a similar line-up, without the two-door sedan. The station wagon series included the luxury Colony Park four-door, nine-passenger model; intermediate Voyager four-door, nine-passenger and two-door, six-passenger models; and three low-priced Commuter models including two four-door models, a nine-passenger version, and one two-door six-passenger wagon. All Mercury station wagons used the same base bodies.

Primary differences in the Montclair and Monterey series was Montclair's minor trim additions and its automatic transmission; Monterey had a standard three-speed manual. Two engines were available: the 255-horsepower, 312 cubic-inch Safety Surge V8 and the 290 hp, 368 cubic-inch Turnpike Cruiser V8. Overall length of the Mercury was in-

*Despite a completely new bodyshell in 1957, Mercury sales were poor. This Monterey Phaeton two-door hardtop was one model in Mercury's lowest-priced line.*

creased from 206 inches in '56 to 211 in '57. Height was lowered to 56.5 inches from the 58.6 and 60.6 inches in the various models the previous year.

### Cruiser's Failure

A FAILURE that prompted a rethinking at Mercury was that of the Turnpike Cruiser. The Cruiser was a forerunner of the Edsel and a harbinger of more bad news. Mercury's "most dramatic expression of Dream-Car design" turned out to be a flat-out bust.

When the car was being planned in 1955, the medium-size market was booming. Mercury executives decided they would attempt to take over that market segment's styling leadership, so they made Mercury a totally new car with its own body shell.

1

Mercury Monterey models, such as the two-door sedan (1), were available with three-speed manual transmission. The Turnpike Cruiser (2, 4) was a marketing disaster. The convertible (3), however, was popular and was raced successfully at Daytona in 150-mile events.

## 1957 Mercury Specifications

| Make and Model | Dimensions | | | | Engines | | Weight lbs. |
| | Wheelbase ins. | Overall Length ins. | Overall Width ins. | Overall Height ins. | 312 cu. in. V8 255 Bhp | 368 cu. in. V8 290 Bhp | |
| --- | --- | --- | --- | --- | --- | --- | --- |
| Montery | 122 | 211.1 | 79.1 | 56.5 | S | 0 | 3925 |
| Montclair | 122 | 211.1 | 79.1 | 56.5 | S | 0 | 3925 |

Key: S: Standard Engine O: Optional Engine

3

They made the Turnpike Cruiser the top-of-the-line model, with "skylight dual-curve" windshield and "retractable, power-operated" back window. Advertising highlighted features such as dual air intake horns over the windshield; quad headlights in large chrome mountings with a small, strange-looking hood over them; "Seat-O-Matic" with controls that lodged the driver's seat automatically into positions A-E and 1-7 according to his preference; a flat-top steering wheel; and steel rods that extended from the top corners of the windshield out of the dual air intake horns in Flash Gordon fashion. Despite the general interest at the time in science fiction and the future, car buyers did not seem to want moon rockets in their own garages. Only slightly more than 17,000 Turnpike Cruisers

▲ The front end of '57 Mercurys, such as the Montclair Phaeton Sedan, sported hooded headlights and a split front bumper.

The "Mermaid," a specially built Mercury Monterey Roadster, reached a top speed of 159.91 miles per ▼ hour at Daytona.

were built in the 1957 model year and about 6000 the following year before production was stopped.

The '57 model Cruiser was available in four-door and two-door hardtops and a special-order convertible announced to the public in December 1956. The convertible was a replica of the model named to be the official pace car for the Indianapolis 500 Race the following Memorial Day. The two-door hardtop, weighing in at a little more than 4000 pounds, retailed at about $3700, while the four-door hardtop, at almost the same weight, cost $100 more. The convertible offered an optional Continental spare and rear bumper extension.

Pushbuttons were in vogue, so the all-new Cruiser went with the times, offering a pushbutton transmission selector on the dash and pushbutton con-

| ▲ The Mercury Convertible Cruiser did not sell any better than its equally gimmicky hardtop counterparts in 1957. | Convertible Mercury Cruisers were available with an extended rear bumper and exterior-mounted spare ▼ tire. |

trol for lowering the back window into the rear deck compartment. Other new features included 14-inch wheels and air-cushion rear suspension. Yet even the customer-accepted features could not save the Cruiser, destined from the start to be just a futuristic failure.

Before the 1958 models were introduced, Mercury was rejoined with Lincoln under the leadership of James J. Nance. Ben D. Mills, formerly Lincoln Division general manager, became assistant general manager in the revised organization. The bold experiment that included the separation of the division, the Turnpike Cruiser and the Edsel was a grim memory. The mistakes had hurt, but not enough to prevent a strong management team from rebuilding.

# STUDEBAKER- PACKARD CORPORATION

IN 1957 Studebaker-Packard was in deep trouble. The ill-conceived combination, created when declining Packard purchased fatally ailing Studebaker in 1954, had not produced the desired result: a fourth rival to the industry's Big Three. Although Studebaker had scooped the field with the first new postwar cars by a prewar company in 1946, it had failed to meet the need for product improvement by the time the postwar seller's market turned to a buyer's market in 1951. Production, which had peaked at over 268,000 in calendar 1950, declined to just 85,000 in the merger year. Studebaker's share of the market during early 1956 was just 1.56 percent.

Packard, although well-off financially until 1954, also faced a grim future. With its 1945 decision to continue offering a range of medium-priced cars in the tradition of the depression-born One Twenty, Packard's luxury aura began to wear thin. A grand old tradition was thus sacrificed for short-range profit that saw alleged Packards selling for as much as $1000 under certain Cadillac models. Both Cadillac and Lincoln reestablished themselves as unadulterated luxury cars after the war—Packard did not. There were other problems, too. The lack of a management retirement program prevented new blood from rising high at Packard, and the 1951 models, which originated in the design stage in 1948, were very old hat by 1954.

**New President at Packard**

IN 1952 PACKARD's aging president Hugh Ferry brought in as his successor James J. Nance, ace salesman-executive who had done so much for the Hotpoint appliance firm. Nance, Ferry hoped, would turn Packard around and rescue its future. Nance began with thunder and lightning, making massive staff changes and giving voluminous directives, numberless press conferences and pep talks. "The industry's watching us," he told his key managers after a few months of this. "Now, by God, let's not disappoint 'em."

Nance soon approached Studebaker about the idea of a merger. Not until recently has it been suggested that this move embodied much more than a simple merger of the two companies. According to Mr. Nance, he had acted with the encouragement of Nash's George Mason. Mason had a grand scheme in mind. While Packard was absorbing Studebaker, Nash would merge with Hudson; then the two units would themselves merge to unite the independents under one huge corporation that could meet the Big Three squarely in every marketplace. "I'm sure I wouldn't have wanted (Studebaker)," Nance said, "if I didn't see them as part of a bigger picture."

Nance believes that the scheme fell apart immediately after Mason's untimely death in October, 1954. Mason's successor, George Romney, deciding to go it alone with his popular Rambler, dismissed thoughts of a Studebaker-Packard-Nash-Hudson tie-up. By this time, of course, Nance had already picked up Studebaker. Time and experience revealed that this was a company Packard might well have done without.

With an obsolete, high-overhead South Bend, Indiana, factory, a recalcitrant (some said spoiled) labor force, aging styling and engineering, and a tenuous dealer network, Studebaker's share of the S-P operation was in dire straits from the start. While not noted during purchase negotiations, its

This quarter-scale model of the proposed 1957 Packard shows what could have been if financial problems had not plagued the company.

books ultimately revealed a break-even point of about 200,000 cars—an output Studebaker had not achieved since 1951.

Nance, who ran the show as president and chief operating officer (Studebaker's Paul G. Hoffman was given an innocuous board chairmanship),soon realized that a divided team of South Bend and Detroit workshops was no way to achieve essential economies. But his efforts to come to terms with Studebaker's overhead and difficult labor situation were too little, or too late.

**Finance or Fold**

BY MID-1956, when other companies were introducing their 1957 models at long-lead previews, Studebaker-Packard was said to have enough resources to keep operating only another two months. Attempts to get new financing from conventional quarters failed. Fortune pictured a tired Nance, walking the streets of New York's financial district on a vain search for capital. Efforts to bring South Bend's towering deficits into line were ineffective. Talks with other auto companies about mergers—both Ford and Chrysler were consulted— were fruitless. First quarter 1956 sales were only 85 percent of the previous year's, and the S-P market percentage was only 2.2.

A problem not of its own making was the aggravated retail competition resulting from the still-smoking Ford-Chevy sales duel which had seen those two companies shipping unwanted cars to dealers by the truckload. The dealers discounted to the limit in order to unload them—to the peril of the independent dealers, who were nowhere as well fixed. "Obviously," said once-confident James J. Nance, "we are confronted with an extremely difficult situation . . . no reasonable and feasible solution to the company's problems is being left unexplored."

The final answer came in the form of old-line aircraft builder Curtiss-Wright, which purchased controlling interest in Studebaker-Packard in July, 1956. S-P's destiny now lay with Curtiss-Wright's feisty president Roy Hurley, who candidly admitted he was interested in it at least partially for a tax write-off. Hurley swept out the Nance managers; Nance himself hung around only long enough to get his top people placed elsewhere.

Roy Hurley moved fast. The tired Packard plant on East Grand Boulevard, Detroit, had produced its last 1956 Packard and Clippers in the same month Curtiss-Wright took over. So dilapidated that a one-ton forklift was not allowed to operate above the first floor, the building was relegated to storage and minor shop work. The newly built Packard engine plant in Utica, Michigan, was allocated to whatever defense business could be drummed up from a sympathetic Eisenhower Administration. All automotive production was centered in South Bend. Harold Churchill, longtime Studebaker engineer, was put in charge there.

## Three Phase Survival Program

CHURCHILL'S PROGRAM for the 1957 Studebaker-Packard operation encompassed three important phases: facelifting the Studebaker line enough to salvage a reasonable market percentage —without spending too much money; dualling 1400 Packard and 2100 Studebaker dealerships which had survived 1956; and coming to grips with the problem of what to do about the 1957 Packard.

Progress was made with the dualling program; over 700 dealers were handling both makes by the end of 1956. Churchill expressed confidence that the dealers he had left were determined loyalists who would support the automotive program, whatever it was.

The program wasn't much; they could not afford extensive changes. Line leader for Studebaker was a modestly facelifted Golden Hawk, running South Bend's 289 cubic-inch V8 engine with a McCulloch supercharger and 275 horsepower. The rest of the line was only mildly facelifted, and Churchill hoped the sporty Hawks could support it. For Packard, Churchill promised "the finest car in the highest price field," a car based on the Packard Predictor show model—but only for 1958. This, of course, never materialized. The money simply was not there. As for the 1957 Packard, its shape and substance remained a mystery until late in 1956. Many people predicted that it would not emerge at all.

The word that best describes Studebaker-Packard for 1957 is "rationalization." Realizing that the Nance-Mason dream of full market competition with the Big Three was not in the cards, S-P aimed to be a builder of special cars for specific markets, while leaving full-tilt volume competition to the larger companies. At the same time S-P embarked on a plan to sell Mercedes-Benz cars through its dealerships, although Churchill carefully pointed out that this was "Roy Hurley's baby."

For the collector and enthusiast, the 1957 cars of Studebaker-Packard are good examples of *in extremis* desperation by a typically troubled independent in the face of a Big Three avalanche. In that they were not unlike American Motors of the late Sixties and Seventies. Lacking the money, or the sources of it, to fully reengineer its line, S-P retrenched with familiar engineering and bodywork, while trying to implement a lot of clever styling and engineering features, like the Hawks, finned drum brakes, variable-rate coil springs and variable-ratio steering. The result was cars that were usually interesting, sometimes remarkably good. The 1957 Hawks are held by some as the best examples of the species, the best integrated stylewise and the most luxuriously equipped. The Packards that finally emerged for 1957 are interesting for their determined resemblance to the Detroit Packards of 1955-56. They were not Packards in the 1956 sense, of course, but they were certainly the best possible Studebakers.

From history's standpoint, the cars represent a more dismal story: the difficulty of trying to survive as an independent against rivals who often make more money than whole nations, and often spend more on a facelift than a small firm spends on a complete restyle. Studebaker-Packard stayed alive in 1957—but just barely. When it finally succumbed (as Studebaker Corporation) in 1966, it was to the same disease manifest in 1957.

# STUDEBAKER

THE STUDEBAKER line for 1957 was as facelifted as the faltering resources of a company in severe financial straits could manage. Most reviewers held that these minor modifications were an improvement.

The regular passenger line was almost certainly upgraded to a "more important" look having the appearance of a new model; the sporty Hawk series had new identity at the rear with bold, concave tailfins. The top-of-the-line Golden Hawk was now powered by a supercharged Studebaker 289 cubic-inch V8 instead of the heavy Packard 352 of the year before. Unique features held over from 1956 included the Safety-Eye revolving speedometer (on all non-Hawks); the engine-turned aluminum dash with full Stewart-Warner instrumentation (on Hawks); South Bend's useful Twin-Traction differential; and the Hill Holder, a device to keep the manual-shift cars from rolling backwards when stopped on a hill. The automatic was Borg-Warner's three-speed "Flight-O-Matic"—as good a clutchless gearbox as was available at the time.

The Hawks were the brightest spots in the 1957 Studebaker lineup. The previous year's range of Flight Hawks, Sky Hawks, Power Hawks, and Golden Hawks was reduced to just two models; the new Silver Hawk and Golden Hawk. They both were well styled and the looks of one complemented the

1

2

Predecessor to the ponycars of the Sixties, the 1957 Silver Hawk (1) had sporty European styling and seating for a family of four. Studebaker's Golden Hawk (2), with its 289 cubic-inch super-charged V8, would have put many ponycars out to pasture. The '57 engine developed 275 hp. A family sedan, the 1957 Commander (3) came in two-and four-door models in standard and deluxe versions. It was powered by a 259 cubic-inch V8.

3

*The President Classic was the only sedan mounted on the Hawk's longer 120.5-inch wheelbase. All other 1957 Studebaker sedans came on a 116.5-inch wheelbase chassis.*

other. Both Hawks were attractively trimmed inside and out. The Silver Hawk offered two engines: the timeless L-head Six, now producing 101 horsepower; and the 289 cubic-inch V8 of up to 225 horsepower (with optional four-barrel carburetor). The same McCulloch supercharger that powered all 1957 Packard Clippers was used with the Golden Hawk's 289, resulting in the same 275 hp its predecessor had offered the previous year. The 289 was a heavy engine by comparison to rival V8s in the same displacement class, but it was 120 pounds lighter than the 1956 Golden Hawk's 352 incher; as a result, the car handled much better than it had before.

Elimination of the Packard engine was an obvious financial advantage, but Studebaker-Packard insisted that the need for better handling was the true reason for the 352's demise. The latter had provided more than adequate performance, but its weight had induced sloppy handling; in addition, its Ultramatic transmission was 20 pounds heavier than Studebaker's store-bought Borg-Warner. The new Golden Hawk's weight distribution was 57-43 front-to-rear, instead of 60-40 as in 1956, and the car took corners handily while retaining some understeer. The Golden Hawk driver still might not have been able to tail a well-driven Austin Healey down a twisty road, but he could negotiate the curves with a degree of finesse unavailable in '56.

## Hawk Performance

PERFORMANCE WAS as good as before, and in some areas better. One magazine found the '57 Golden Hawk to be six miles per hour faster in the quarter mile than its predecessor, at 87 vs 81 mph. The Golden Hawk was also beautifully equipped: its white-on-black gauges (including tachometer and clock with sweep second hand) boldly faced the driver, its minor functions were controlled by positive-acting toggle switches; its semibucket seats were done up in deeply cushioned vinyl.

The Silver Hawk was conservatively trimmed in comparison—sans tach, with bench seats in a combination of cloth and vinyl—but it was still a lush-looking car. In body style it was a five-window coupe instead of a hardtop; and its two-tone paint style, using fins and lower body for the second color, was less imaginative. But it was a tighter Hawk thanks to its extra roof pillars, and it offered lively performance with its 225 hp unblown V8 or good economy if the Six was specified. The latter combination cost only $2142, making the Silver Hawk Six one of 1957's best buys.

The 1957 Hawks, incidentally, represented the first efforts of new South Bend and Detroit stylists, and were the first Studebakers since before World War II that were not at least partly styled by Raymond Loewy. True, they did use the old Loewy

# 1957 Studebaker Specifications

| Make and Model | Dimensions | | | | Engines | | | | | | Weight lbs. |
|---|---|---|---|---|---|---|---|---|---|---|---|
| | Wheelbase ins. | Overall Length ins. | Overall Width ins. | Overall Height ins. | 186 cu. in. Six 101 Bhp. | 259 cu. in. V8 180 Bhp. | 259 cu. in. V8 195 Bhp. | 289 cu. in. V8 210 Bhp. | 289 cu. in. V8 225 Bhp. | 289 cu. in. V8 275 Bhp. | |
| Commander V8 | 116.5 | 202.4 | 75.8 | 59.8 | — | S | O | — | O | — | 3140 |
| President | 116.5 | 202.4 | 75.8 | 59.8 | — | — | O | S | O | — | 3205 |
| President Classic | 120.5 | 206.4 | 75.8 | 59.8 | — | — | O | O | S | — | 3270 |
| Champion | 116.5 | 202.4 | 75.8 | 59.8 | S | — | — | — | — | — | 2810 |
| Silver Hawk Six | 120.5 | 204 | 71.3 | 55 | S | — | — | — | — | — | 2790 |
| Silver Hawk V8 | 120.5 | 204 | 71.3 | 55 | — | — | S | O | O | — | 3185 |
| Golden Hawk | 120.5 | 204 | 71.3 | 55 | — | — | — | — | — | S | 3400 |

**Key:** S: Standard Engine  O: Optional Engine

coupe body, and their tailfins were an obvious sop to sales; but they were gracefully designed nonetheless. Wisely, stylists retained the Hawk's most distinguishing features of 1956: the classic-type egg-crate grille and free-standing parking lights. The 1957 Hawks were and still are good-looking cars. And because of their relatively low production, they are highly sought after by collectors.

## Styling Rationale

ACCORDING TO South Bend's admen, if nobody else, the lack of major restyling for 1957 was not the result of financial chaos but of a market survey. Most people, South Bend said, had found the 1956 styling "very acceptable." (No such reaction is indicated by sales figures: 116,333 in 1955; 69,593 in

The 1957 President Broadmoor station wagon featured an extended rear bumper. Other '57 wagons included the Provincial V8 four-door, Parkview V8 two-door and Pelham Six two-door.

1956). For whatever reason, modifications to the non-Hawk line were slight: grilles were stretched across the entire front end, and the front bumper dipped in the middle to accentuate the grillework. The 1956 President model had been garish, with a multitude of chrome side strips, so in 1957 the single chrome spear across the front two-thirds of the car was a sign of design cleanliness. At the rear, Presidents sported a forward-pointed section for the two-toning to match the roof color; Champion and Commander Deluxe models used a single fore-to-aft chrome strip; and Custom versions had a single strip from front fender to mid-wheelbase. Fins were disdained for the non-Hawk line, although the rear fender was built up to house large, three-segment taillights enclosing back-up, tail and turn signal lamps.

Interiors for 1957 were thoroughly revised, and some offered exceptional quality for cars in the price class, especially those of the 120.5-inch wheelbase President Classic (ex-Land Cruiser) sedan. Studebaker continued to use full instrumentation; the bathroom-scale-type speedometer presented only one speed at a time in a little window and changed from green to red as speed mounted.

By 1957, the economy car swing was on and Volkswagen sales were increasing. Studebaker sought a spot in this market with the Scotsman, a full-size car of severe specifications: cardboard and paint substituted for vinyl and chrome in all too many places. The Scotsman was a failure. It made no inroads in the economy car market, partly because it was so plain, and partly because it was an unknown quantity to purchasers who liked the Chevy One Fifty. At perhaps $100 more, the Chevrolet was considered a sure thing.

**Sales Droop**

CONSIDERING ITS poor showing in 1956, Studebaker should have done well in 1957—the rest of the industry did. Instead it sold 7000 fewer cars in '57, although the Hawk line was up by 5000 units. Such results were symbolic of Studebaker-Packard's general decline, its dim prospects for the future, the lack of faith in them by the consumer, the diminishing dealerships, and the fear among prospects that they might end up with an "orphan" a few years hence.

At this very time, remember, a 1950 Studebaker that had cost $1500 when new was retailing for about $275, against $100 more than that for the equivalent Ford and about $200 more for the equivalent Chevrolet. The cars were further troubled by their lack of market appeal. There had been no convertible since 1952, the only hardtop was the expensive Golden Hawk, and there was no money to tool for a four-door hardtop. All these body styles were subject to major sales thrusts by the Big Three. The 289 V8 engine was old and overweight, being kept in the horsepower race only with a supercharger, soldered on because S-P could not afford to design a new lightweight engine like Chevy's 265-283 or Plymouth's 277-301. Such factors could not be overcome, even by the factory where, as S-P said, "Pride of Workmanship Comes First."

# PACKARD

THE PACKARD planned for 1957 bore no resemblance to what finally appeared under that title. Contemplated in the salad days of 1954 and 1955, when the future still looked promising and business was fair, was a whole new line of long, chiseled, streamlined Packards—Caribbeans, Patricians, Clippers—along the lines of the Packard Predictor. This narrow-grilled 1956 one-off car invoked several ideas later repeated by other companies—the tall, mock-classic radiator grille of traditional Packard looks; sculpted, almost knife-edge styling; comprehensive electrical assists operating such items as hidden headlights and retractable, reverse-canted rear window; and rakish tail fins. By early 1957, tooling-up for these cars was a financial impossibility, and the new generation of big Packards was permanently abandoned.

In the view of Harold Churchill, however, some sort of Packard would have to be provided for 1957. The dealers needed it, and there was the question of dealer franchises, which had promised it. To Churchill, even if the planned 1958s appeared on schedule, an interim '57 was necessary. It would have been difficult to preserve the continuity of the Packard name and revive it after the name had not appeared for 12 months. Although Henry Ford managed this when he switched from Model T to Model A, it was quite another ball game; Packard now had none of the fierce loyalty and market dominance that Ford had.

With consolidation of automotive production in South Bend, the solution to Churchill's problem was obvious: take the largest Studebaker chassis, the President Classic, mate it to the most powerful Golden Hawk V8 engine (the big Packard V8s disappeared after 1956), graft on as much family resemblance as possible to the previous Packards and Clippers—and sell the model for several hundred dollars more than the President Classic to avoid fraternal competition. Churchill proposed such a car to the S-P board in August, 1956, estimating a tooling cost of only $1.1 million and break-even between 4000 and 6000 units. The board and dealers accepted it; indeed, they had no choice. With few weeks to do the job, stylist Dick Teague performed well.

*Built to reflect the future Packard styling, the Predictor was a show car. It sported an electrically operated rear window, concealed headlamps, roll-top roof sections and a windshield that flowed into the roof. Seat cushions were reversible, with fabric- and leathered-covered sides.*

Saddled with financial woes that prevented a totally new Packard from appearing in 1957, Harold Churchill decided to piece together the Packard Clipper from previous-model parts.

## Packard Clipper

AN EARLY marketing decision—probably the right one—was to call this new '57 the "Packard Clipper," instead of just "Packard," which it wasn't by any stretch of the imagination, or "Clipper" which would have signalled the end of Packard. Included were remnants of the 1956 models: steeply angled, tapered taillights from the past year's Packard Executive; a Clipper-type dashboard with leftover '56 instruments; a narrowed version of 1956's bright metal side molding; and fashionably hooded headlights. Parts bins supplied diverse identification: Clipper ship's wheels, Clipper script, a 1955 hood ornament, and twin radio antennas mounted on the rear fenders. It was too soon for dual headlights and too late in the tooling program for tailfins, so these excrescences thankfully were avoided. The result was an acceptable medium-priced Clipper, surprisingly close in dimension to the 1956 version.

The dimensional similarity often goes unnoticed, but the sedan wheelbase was 120.5 inches, for example, against 122 for the previous Clipper. The '57 sedan was nearly 212 inches long, versus 214 for the '56, and its overall width of 77 inches was only an inch less. Even in the horsepower department, no loss was suffered. The blown 289 V8

produced the same 275 horsepower that had been offered in the 352 cubic-inch V8-powered 1956 Clipper Custom.

Inside and out, all manner of luxuries were standard equipment: quality linen tweed and color-coordinated vinyl upholstery, deep carpet, padded dashboard, foam rubber seat cushions, back-up lights and clock. The options included

Steeply angled and tapered taillights of the '57 Packard Clipper were remnants of the 1956 Packard Executive.

power windows, brakes, steering and seats; with a $440 air conditioning unit. By today's standards the 1957 Packard was a mite chromey, perhaps even heroically overdecorated. By the standards of 1957, however, it was a relatively tasteful concoction.

S-P flyers advertised the new Packard as invoking "a new age of functional elegance, the best of two automotive worlds." Here was all the richness "of the Packard way," combined with "versatile supercharged power (the blower freewheeled economically until 3000 rpm) without the usual penalties in excess weight and lost economy." It was not, incidentally, cheap. At $3212 for the four-door Town Sedan, and $3384 for the Country Sedan, it was higher priced than all the 1956 Clippers, and close to Packard territory.

Lacking new basics, the engineers did their best to equip the car with the most advanced components available. The automatic transmission offered as standard equipment was Borg-Warner's Flight-O-Matic, a three-speed with torque converter. Twin-Traction limited slip differential, a South Bend item, was optional at slight extra cost, and three rear-axle ratios were available. The suspension did not use torsion bars, as per the 1956 Packards and Clipper Customs, but the cars were equipped with variable-rate front coil springs which compressed differently depending on the load. Variable-ratio steering, a first for S-P in the American industry, provided a quick steering ratio for high-speed motoring and a lower one for parking. The finned brake drums were generally held to be the best of their type in the business.

Although Studebaker-Packard produced 3940 sedans against just 869 wagons, special attention must be given the latter. First Packard station wagon since 1950, the 1957 Country Sedan was a quality car for luxurious hauling, with more than adequate cargo capacity. Remarkably, it appears directly related to the Town Sedan, despite being built on a smaller wheelbase. It did not feature variable-ratio front coil springs; however, it did use two-stage leafs at the rear. Air conditioning was not offered.

*Motor Trend* had been monitoring the S-P corporate situation closely since financial problems became obvious, and soon assured the public that a 1957 Packard was indeed coming. When the magazine got one for test, they did the 0-60 mph sprint in 11 seconds flat, and concluded that performance was really excellent. The 1957 Packard, *MT* concluded, was "readily distinguishable from the Studebaker." The editors also pointed out that the sharing of a Studebaker body "should cause little concern . . . the use of one body shell over two and even three different nameplates is an old Detroit habit, too . . . the driver who wishes something off the beaten path in '57 at least owes it to himself to closely examine and drive the new Clipper."

S-P itself added to the final publicity barrage: "If

## 1957 Packard Clipper Specifications

| Make and Model | Dimensions | | | | Engines | Weight lbs. |
| | Wheelbase Ins. | Overall Length Ins. | Overall Width Ins. | Overall Height Ins. | 289 cu. in. V8 275 Bhp | |
|---|---|---|---|---|---|---|
| Clipper | 120.5 | 211.8 | 77 | 60.1 | S | 3270 |

**Key:** *S: Standard Engine*

you believe that fine styling must be matched by superior workmanship in your next car . . . if you expect engineering advances beyond horsepower alone—the Packard Clipper is your kind of car. Behind its proud Packard grille is cradled not merely high horsepower, but a totally new performance for every driving situation. Within its trim, taut lines is a degree of luxury and spaciousness that only a Packard Clipper provides for your personal comfort. Every detail, down to the thickness and strength of the steel body panels, carries with it a Packard Clipper quality that is unsurpassed by even the most expensive luxury cars!"

### Tradition and Skill

WHILE HAROLD Churchill did not produce "the finest car in the highest price field," he can be credited with an old automan's love of tradition by continuing a well-respected name—and designer Dick Teague can be credited with a degree of skill that left the 1957 Studebaker-based Packard closely reminiscent of the Packards that had gone before. The 1958 Packards, last of the breed, were not of the same order. With huge, ungainly tail fins, wide Martha Raye grilles, and ugly pod-type dual headlight units grafted onto one-headlight fenders for the sake of keeping up with competition, they were garish in the extreme. For anyone who likes Studebakers, the 1957 Packards are among the best examples of how luxurious a Studebaker can be—a sort of ultimate for the Fifties.

Fortunately, the cars are available today at reasonable prices. The sedans, of course, predominate, but wagons do come on the market from time to time. The cars are recognized by all national Studebaker and Packard clubs, giving them a kind of dual interest not applicable to earlier models. Mechanical parts are easy to find, while body parts are as scarce as production would lead one to expect. Despite the resemblances, few body components are interchangeable with earlier Packards and Clippers.